Beautiful
Beaded & Embroidered
FABRIC

Beautiful
Beaded & Embroidered
FABRIC

Cindy Gorder

Sterling Publishing Co., Inc.

New York

Prolific Impressions Production Staff:
Editor in Chief: Mickey Baskett
Copy Editor: Phyllis Mueller
Graphics: Cindy Gorder
Styling: Lenos Key
Photography: Jerry Mucklow
Administration: Jim Baskett

Library of Congress Cataloging-in-Publication Data

Gorder, Cindy
  Beautiful beaded & embroidered fabric / Cindy Gorder
          p. cm.
  Includes index.
  ISBN-13: 978-1-4027-2451-0
  ISBN-10: 1-4027-2451-9
1. Beadwork--Patterns. 2. Embroidery--Patterns. I. Title. II. Title: Beautiful beaded and embroidered fabric

TT860.G67 2006
746.5--dc22
                                                                    2006021021

2 4 6 8 10 9 7 5 3 1

Published by Sterling Publishing Co., Inc.
387 Park Avenue South, New York, NY 10016

© 2006 by Prolific Impressions, Inc.

Distributed in Canada by Sterling Publishing
c/o Canadian Manda Group, 165 Dufferin Street, Toronto, Ontario, Canada M6K 3H6
Distributed in the United Kingdom by GMC Distribution Services,
Castle Place, 166 High Street, Lewes, East Sussex, England BN7 1XU
Distributed in Australia by Capricorn Link (Australia) Pty. Ltd.
P.O. Box 704, Windsor, NSW 2756, Australia

Printed in China
All rights reserved

Sterling ISBN-13: 978-1-4027-2451-0
          ISBN-10: 1-4027-2451-9

For information about custom editions, special sales, premium and corporate purchases, please contact Sterling Special Sales Department at 800-805-5489 or specialsales@sterlingpub.com.

Thank You

to the following manufacturers for providing materials for making the projects in this book:

For hot-fix rhinestones & setting tool:
Creative Crystal
creative-crystal.com

For metallic embroidery thread:
Facets(tm) bead-like yarn
Kreinik Mfg. Co.
www.kreinik.com

For ribbons, fibers and trims:
Embellishments!
www.fibergoddess.com

Flights of Fancy Boutique
www.flightsoffancy.com

For clip art:
Sterling/Chapelle
Sterling Publishing Co. Inc
www.sterlingpub.com

The Vintage Workshop™
www.thevintageworkshop.com

About the Author

Cindy Gorder is a professional graphic artist and freelance designer of needle and paper crafts. Many of her projects have been published in craft magazines and she is the author of three other books: *Greeting Cards in an Afternoon* (Sterling, 2001), *Fancy Work with Beading* (Design Originals, 2000), and *Beaded Crazy Quilting* (KP Books, 2005). She is the editor and graphic designer of *Decorating Digest Craft & Home Projects,* a subscriber-based craft magazine published six times a year.

Encouraged from an early age to indulge creative expression, Cindy has tried many mediums and particularly enjoys those that include beads, fancy fabrics, altered textiles, fibers, paper, and digital designing.

This book is dedicated to Dick – husband, best friend, partner, and love of my life.

Acknowledgments

I thank my mother and grandmothers, who showed me the magic of using needle and thread; both parents who, by their examples, taught me to embrace creativity; and my encouraging and patient editor, Mickey Baskell.

Contents

112

116

100

Introduction

I think I've always been drawn to beads, but when I was growing up they weren't readily available, at least not in my small rural town. I did learn to sew, however, and from my grandmother I learned a little embroidery, but eventually I drifted away from those things, until a job working in the craft industry took me to a trade show in the early '90s. In those days, even though the shows weren't open to the public, vendors were allowed to sell products outright in their booths. Out of the hundreds (if not a thousand) booths at that show, there was one vendor selling beads. One whole wall of the booth was hung with hanks of seed and bugle beads of every color imaginable. I had never seen anything like it, all those beads together in one place! Like a crow with a shiny object, I was mesmerized. As I went about my work at that show, I made it a point to go by that booth every chance I got.

On the last day, I drummed up the courage to approach the vendor and ask his prices. I figured I could afford a couple of hanks and two of the dazzling crystal cabochons in his glass display case. I bought them, completely unaware this would be a defining moment in my life—the turning of a new leaf, so to speak.

The first thing I did when I unpacked back at home was admire my exciting purchases. Then it dawned on me – I didn't have a clue about how to actually make something with those beads! When I tried to imagine how one might work with the beads on the hanks, the first hurdle was figuring out how to keep them from falling off the string once the string was released from the hank. (Without a bookstore or the Internet available, I was completely stumped! This was years before the first bead shop appeared in my area.) The beads went into storage for a few years before I discovered that beads have to be removed from the strings of the hanks in order to use them!

In 1995, I signed up for a crazy quilting class and in two evenings I learned enough about embroidery to start doing the crazy quilting I had long admired. It didn't take long to discover how terrific the threadwork looked with the addition of beads! By then a couple of bead shops had opened for business in the small city an hour away and my serious pursuit of beads began. Luckily for me, beading was enjoying a rise in popularity all across the nation and beads were becoming more available.

Today, even if you live in a rural area like I do, you can get just about any bead you want from numerous Internet vendors. But there's still something magical about seeing and touching them in a store or at a bead show. Bead shows abound, and if you've never been to one, I highly recommend the experience of seeing a wide variety of beads in one place.

And speaking of acquiring beads…

Years of collecting has given me a stash of beads and embroidery threads that allow me to start a project as soon as the idea occurs. All projects in this book were created from beads I acquired here and there—even if I could remember where I found a specific bead, it's possible that source may no longer carry the particular item in its inventory. But chances are quite good someone has that particular size and color bead for sale (unless it was a vintage bead—then all bets are off). It's your choice—you can spend a lot of time looking for the exact same beads I used, or you can make it easy on yourself and use beads to which you have easy access (such as your own stash!). I say this so you know that when I list a size, color, and finish for a seed bead or rocaille I used in a project, it is only that—what I used, and not what you must use.

About this book…

I've included information about beads and beading supplies and some tips for working with them. You'll also find instructions and illustrations for the beading and embroidery stitches and 20 beading projects with step-by-step instructions, numerous photographs, and all the necessary patterns. Feel free to make substitutions in the projects you create, and to take some artistic and creative license. Give yourself permission to experiment—make your creations uniquely yours, and you'll enjoy the opportunity to use beads you love and have at hand.

Cindy Gorder

Beading Supplies

With only a few beads and some embroidery floss or specialty thread, you can create exquisite works of art. Your supplies will take up little space, and your project is very portable. This section gives information on the types of beads used to create the beaded embroidery projects in this book and the tools and supplies you'll use to work with them.

Beads

The projects are embellished with readily available seed and bugle beads. Some projects use a few decorative specialty beads for accent. In the project supplies lists, the phrase **decorative beads** refers to these specialty beads used in the project – not the seed or bugle beads. In some projects, I've used buttons and pearls as well. All are excellent choices for embellishing fabric surfaces.

SEED BEADS

Seed beads (also called **rocailles**) are the mainstay of every project in this book. Made of glass, they come in myriad colors, finishes, and cuts. They are round or oblate in shape (fatter in diameter than they are long). Japanese or Czech beads are the kind most readily available and of good quality.

Sizes: The most common size is 11; but sizes range from 22 (the smallest) to 15, 8, or size 5 (5/0 - the largest seed bead). Beads with higher numbers are smaller in size. If you are buying a size 11 bead, you may see the size designation listed in several ways – as size 11, or 11/0, or 11°. They are all the same size of bead. Sizes vary slightly; however, size 6 (6/0) is about 3.3 mm or 10 beads per inch. A size 11 bead measures about 1.8 mm in diameter and there may be as many as 20 beads per inch.

How they are sold: Seed beads are sold in a variety of containers, from small packets and bags to large tubes, tiny blister packs to hanks (beads on temporary string carriers), and sometimes measured by weight in grams. Hanks of (usually) 12 strands contain larger quantities and are often the most economically priced. The good news is that most projects require only a very small amount of seed beads—perhaps a teaspoon or two. If more than that is required, the quantity is noted in the list of supplies. (It was a challenge to specify exact amounts.) My seed bead stash includes beads in every kind of container and quantity.

Color & Finish: The beads can be transparent or opaque. Transparent seed beads have a beautiful luster that is the result of the interior hole being lined with a metallic color, or sometimes pink or blue. An exterior metallic coating is sometimes added to the beads – these beads are called "AB" beads – or "Aurora Borealis."

Seed beads are sold in many sizes and containers.

Bugle beads shown in some of their numerous sizes and containers.

BUGLE BEADS

Bugle beads are tubular in shape and are perhaps the second-most common type of glass bead. They have the same size designations and color varieties as seed beads. They may be round or have six (or more) flat sides. Like seed beads, they are sold in a wide variety of colors, sizes, and finishes.

The **micro tube** is an extremely tiny tubular bead. Don't be intimidated by their very small size—it makes them very suitable for a project where smooth curves are desirable. The ones I have seen are extremely shiny so they look sparkly and glittery when they are stitched on fabric. To work with them, you'll need a needle small enough to fit through them (size 15 or 16), very good lighting, and perhaps a magnifying aid.

Bead Storage

STORING LOOSE BEADS

When you start buying and using beads, it's inevitable that you'll have beads you haven't used yet and that there will be leftovers. You can store partially used strands and any loose beads in clear bags or other specialty containers. (Again, the variety of systems available is impressive.) Tiny zipper-top bags are a nice option; they don't take up a lot of space and you can easily see what's in them. Because eventually they will likely come apart at the seams, be diligent about replacing them as needed.

A necktie rack is a handy option for storing beads on hanks.

STORING & USING HANKS

I have many hanks of beads. I found they take up a lot of room if I try to store them in containers along with smaller quantities of loose beads so I purchased a tie rack (the kind with rows of pegs used in a closet to hang up individual neckties), and I use it to store my bead hanks. They're colorful and fun to look at, too, just like in the store. If you use a rack for storage, make sure the knots in the hanks are very secure before hanging them up.

The thread used for hanks is intended for temporary storage, not end use. To use beads from a hank, remove them from the strand, leaving the rest intact if you want to store them that way. TIP: To get unused beads back on the string for storage, use a loop-type dental floss threader.

Needles

With a variety of sizes of needles on hand, you will be prepared for any embellishment task.

Use **embroidery needles** with sharp tips for embroidery stitches. The eye needs to be large enough to easily thread with embroidery cotton. Depending on your surface, a slightly larger needle may be easier to manipulate.

Beading needles come in a range of sizes—the higher size numbers denote smaller needles (like beads). Size 12 needles will work for most size 11 (the most common size) or larger seed beads. Size 15 seed beads and micro-tubes require size 15 needles. Having an assortment of lengths will come in handy—often a short needle is easier to control in a tight or curved space. Long needles are great for making tassels. And medium needles are fairly universal in their utility.

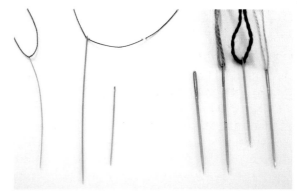

Pictured left to right: *Assorted beading needles and embroidery needles.*

Needles, continued from page 11

Beading needles can become quite bent with use; if they still perform satisfactorily, there's no reason you can't keep using them until they break (and they will eventually break, so keep extras on hand). Forcing a needle through a bead that's too small can accelerate its demise. TIP: Take the time to test a few beads before anchoring thread to fabric to be sure you're using a needle that's small enough for the beads you've chosen.

Use everyday **sewing needles** for hand sewing any time you're using sewing thread.

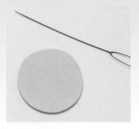

A simple rubber disc called a "needle grabber" makes coaxing a needle through a tight space much easier.

NEEDLE GRABBERS

Not being a thimble-wearer, I have found the small round rubber discs called "needle grabbers" to be an indispensable tool for embroidery and beadwork. They are sold in sewing and quilting notions departments.

Beading Thread

A waxed bead thread works best for me. I find the waxed threads very strong and they don't fray or stretch. They are sold in several sizes and colors; I like size A best. I use this for nearly all my beadwork. You generally only need two colors—white and black—for just about any bead-on-fabric situation. But since I love the color purple, I use purple thread instead of black thread on dark fabrics other than black. When I'm sewing beads to a light-colored fabric, I use white waxed thread.

For many years I used a readily available beading thread that comes in several sizes and lots of colors. I found it to be an excellent choice for stitching beads to fabric, but I also found it could be fairly easily cut by the sharp edges of bugle beads, and that it tended to fray in the needle at the eye and stretch with wear and the weight of beads. (Stretching is not as much of a problem with beaded embroidery as it is with beaded jewelry.)

If your beads are transparent, the thread color will change the bead color somewhat; especially, a dark thread will make the beads look to be a darker color. When I use transparent beads, I use a beading thread color that is compatible with the color of the beads and the fabric.

THREAD FOR BUGLE BEADS

Both regular and waxed beading thread can be cut by the sharp edges of bugle beads. Czech bugle beads are particularly hard on thread; because Japanese bugle beads have smoother edges, they are far less destructive of thread. A solution is to use thread made of Kevlar for sewing bugle beads. It's the same thread used for making bullet-proof vests—just cutting a length of it from the spool will show you how tough it is; only the sharpest of scissors will be up to that task. If you want to use Czech bugles without fear that eventually they'll start falling off, Kevlar thread will do the trick. However, I wouldn't hesitate to use waxed thread with Japanese bugle beads.

Pictured clockwise from top left: *Beading threads—waxed, Kevlar, and unwaxed.*

PREVENTING THREAD TANGLES

Quilter's beeswax or a thread lubricant can help prevent knots, a frequent problem with unwaxed thread; I've heard beeswax even strengthens the thread a bit. I haven't found it necessary to use a lubricant with waxed thread.

Pictured left to right: *Thread lubricant and quilter's beeswax can help prevent thread tangles.*

Embroidery Thread

It's important to choose a color and weight (size) of embroidery thread that will show up against the background fabric so your pretty needlework will stand out. The larger the thread, the smaller the size number. Size 8 pearl cotton is easy to work; size 5 is slightly larger and also quite easy. Depending on how delicate I want the embroidery to look, I generally use size 8 or size 5. Occasionally, I use size 3 thread, which is best suited for larger scale projects. It's also a bit harder to pull through fabric and so requires a larger embroidery needle.

I prefer pearl cotton to six-strand embroidery floss–to me, it just looks prettier. But if you like floss, use it. You can also use crochet or tatting threads in weights comparable to pearl cotton size 8 and size 5. Hand-dyed three-ply cotton needlework threads are lovely. Separate the plies and use each strand individually for most embroidery situations.

One of my favorite specialty threads is metallic fine braid. This type of thread can be a little more difficult to pull through some fabrics only because it's not quite as smooth as cotton; sometimes that can be helped by using a slightly larger embroidery needle and/or a shorter length of thread. I generally prefer size 8 but occasionally use the smaller size 4. (Smaller # = smaller thread.) It is available in many beautiful colors and really makes embroidered work sparkle.

A common rule is to never sew with a length of thread longer than the distance from your hand to your elbow. This makes sense–longer thread takes more effort to pull through. For best results, load your needle with 24" to 30" (or less) of embroidery thread.

Pearl cotton embroidery threads, pictured left to right: *size 8, size 5, size 5 hank, size 3 (hank).*

An assortment of hand-dyed embroidery threads. Thinner ones may be used as is; thicker ones are best separated into strands.

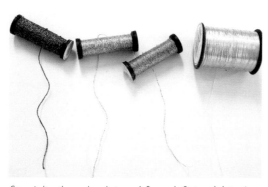

Specialty threads, pictured from left to right, *size 8 fine braid, size 4 fine braid, blending filament, metallic sewing thread.*

BLENDING FILAMENT

This very delicate, fine thread is often used to add sparkle to fine needlework. It can also be used to enhance embroidery (as can metallic sewing thread). When using this thread, use lengths of 12" to 18" to prevent wearing it out with many repeated passes through the fabric.

Sewing Thread

The projects in this book require little, if any, sewing. For general hand sewing, regular sewing thread is all you need. Bead thread can also be used if you don't want to take the time to dig out sewing thread.

Surfaces

I call the objects I purchase to embellish my "surfaces." It's not likely you'll find exactly the same surface I did, so I suggest you use the descriptions and photographs of my surfaces as guides or as a jumping-off point for your own inspiration.

The only criterion you should use to rule out a fabric item is if it cannot be stitched into easily. For example, I purchased a fabric-covered visor, thinking its bill would make a great place for some beading. But because the band was made of a rigid material and at a right angle to the bill, I would have been limited to stitching around the front edge of the bill. I may still do that, but the project is shelved, for now.

If the surface is wearable, take into account how it will be worn, how it will be put on, and how it will be laundered. Some beads aren't colorfast when they go up against dry-cleaning solutions or even water, so test first if that's a concern.

Surfaces, continued from page 13

If the fabric is stretchy and will be stretched when put on or worn (such as a t-shirt), the threads for the embroidery and beadwork could be broken. You can embellish a stretchy fabric, but you have to take the stretching into account when selecting the item. (The shirt in the Pint-Size Princess Outfit project in this book is an example of a "work around" using a cotton single-knit t-shirt.)

Beading Workstation

There are all sorts of ways to keep your beads from getting away from you as you work, from flocked bead boards to a simple piece of felt. When I do beading in my lap (it's great to do in front of the TV!), I use a **felted bead board** atop a lap desk.

I also use a variety of **bead holders**. When I work at a table, my favorite bead holder is an item I purchased from the hardware department that was labeled a "paint edger refill." You can use it straight from the package or use a craft knife to remove the plastic parts that hold it to the intended tool and glue a piece of sheet foam to the back to keep it from sliding around.

Small triangular bead dishes work well for holding decorative beads and larger beads. A tiny scoop is indispensable for picking up leftover loose seed beads and returning them to their containers. To restring beads on hanks for storage, use a plastic loop-type dental floss threader.

Tools & Helpers

Scissors - You will need sewing shears or scissors for cutting fabric. I highly recommend a pair of small scissors for cutting threads, although you could get by with regular sewing shears.

Iron and ironing board, for attaching fusible adhesive and interfacing.

Fabric markers - An air-erasable marker is indispensable for transferring patterns to light- or medium-colored fabrics. Follow the manufacturer's instructions for use, and test the surface first to be sure the marker won't leave a permanent mark.

Quilting pencils come in handy when the pattern lines will be covered with beading–the marks won't fade away like air-erase markers do so you don't have to reapply them if you set aside the project for more than a few hours. White and silver pencils are good for marking dark fabrics.

Pins - Use good quality straight pins with large heads so you can see them easily.

Items for a beading workstation, pictured clockwise from upper left: *My altered paint edger refill used as a bead holder, a small scoop, the paint edger refill as purchased, a loop-type dental floss threader, triangular bead dishes.*

Use quilting pencils or an air-erase marker to transfer patterns.

Straight pins with large heads are easier to see.

Care & Cleaning

No matter how careful you are, beaded and embroidered needlework won't hold up very well to the usual methods of laundering. My best advice is to treat your finished pieces with care to avoid soiling in the first place. Carefully spot clean as necessary, using a damp cloth.

CLOTHING

A garment or wearable piece can sometimes be successfully machine laundered by turning it inside out, placing it in a mesh laundry bag, and washing it in cold water on the gentle cycle. Hand washing is another option. Dry an embellished garment like you would a sweater, smoothing out the wrinkles and placing it flat on a drying rack.

I've had success cleaning an embroidered and beaded garment with a dry-cleaning product made for use in household dryers. Because commercial dry-cleaning can remove the color from your beads and embellishments and permanently damage fibers, I don't recommend it.

DECORATIVE ITEMS

A home decor piece should be kept as free from dirt and spills as possible. If soiling does occur, carefully spot clean with a damp cloth. If dust collects on a wall hanging or pillow, an easy way to clean it without disturbing delicate embellishments is to place a piece of nylon stocking over the end of a vacuum hose and vacuum the dust away. (This also works as a way to pick up spilled beads!)

Stitching Basics

Knotting Thread

I have fallen into the habit of using one kind of knot when I start stitching (an anchor knot) and another type to knot off (end my stitching). This seems more efficient for me, but you certainly could start and end with an anchor knot if you prefer. It makes sense to do that when you have to make your knot on the front of your surface.

Anchor Knot

This is how I start nearly all of my embroidery and bead stitching whenever I begin a new row or change threads. With a little practice you'll learn this method of making a nice, neat knot.

1. Thread the needle and hold it with the thread end hanging down and the needle pointing straight up. *(Photo 1)*

2. With the index finger of the hand holding the needle, hold the tail of the thread against needle and wrap the thread just above your finger around the needle four or five times. *(Photo 2)*

3. Holding the wraps against the needle, carefully pull the needle through, sliding the wraps past the eye and down to the end of the thread. *(Photo 3, Photo 4)* Pull the end to tighten the knot. *(Photo 5)*

4. Trim the tail of the thread close to the knot. *(Photo 6)*

5. Bring up the needle through the fabric from back to front, pulling the knot snugly against the back of the fabric, and begin stitching.

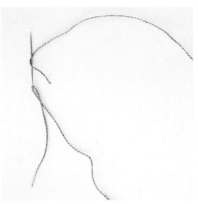

Photo 1 - Thread and needle in position.

Photo 2 - The thread wrapped around the needle.

Photo 3 - Pulling the needle through the wrapped thread.

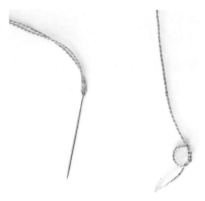

Photo 4 - Sliding the knot to the end of the thread.

Photo 5 - The knot pulled tight.

Photo 6 - Thread is knotted and trimmed.

Knotting Off (Ending Anchor)

Here's how I knot off or end the thread when I'm finished stitching. If you prefer, you can use this anchor stitch in lieu of a knot when you begin stitching–the choice is yours.

1. Take three or four small stitches on top of each other at the back of the fabric. (Photo 7, Photo 8, Photo 9)

2. Trim the thread, leaving thread tail an inch or so long. (This can be done on the front of the fabric if the back is inaccessible. In this case, take an extra stitch or two, and trim The tail close to fabric.)

Photo 7 - Stitching is complete--ready to knot off.

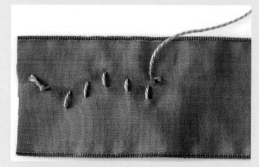

Photo 8 - Small stitches started.

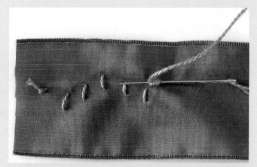

Photo 9 - Taking the final stitch.

Beading Stitches

Single Stitch - Seeds or Bugles

Bring up needle from back of fabric, through bead, and back down through fabric; pull thread snug to remove slack. Move needle at back of fabric to next bead position and repeat.

Side view - Single-stitched seed beads

Side view - Single-stitched bugle beads, end to end

Birds eye view - Single-stitched bugle beads, side by side

Bugles with Seed Beads

The thread rides on the seeds so the sharp edges of the bugle won't wear or cut through.
Bring up thread through fabric and pick up a seed, a bugle and a seed. Go back down near seed bead. Move needle at back of fabric to next stitch position and come up through fabric. Pick up seed, bugle, seed and repeat stitch.

Side view

Backstitch

For a continuous row or line of beads.
First part: Bring up thread from back of fabric. Pick up 6 beads and go back into fabric near last bead, "snugging" the beads together. The beads should lay flat but close together and with no gaps or thread showing.

Second part: Bring needle back up between 4th and 5th stitched beads and go through the last two beads again, emerging from the last stitched bead.

Next stitch: Pick up 6 beads, go back into fabric near end bead, and come back up between 3rd and 2nd bead from stitched end. Go through last 2 stitched beads and pick up 6 more.

   Repeat sequence to create a continuous row.
TIP: Rows can be smoothed or straightened by running the needle and thread back through the entire row.

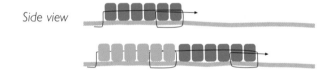

Side view

Backstitch Using Bugles and Seeds

Combining seed beads with bugles in a continuous line.
First part: Bring up thread through fabric and pick up a seed, a bugle and a seed. Go back down near last seed bead.
Second part: Bring needle back up between bugle and last seed stitched and go through those two beads again, emerging from the seed.
Next stitch: Pick up another bugle and seed and repeat sequence.

Side view

Bead Stack

Take needle through one or more beads, ending with a seed bead to serve as a Stop Bead that will hold the bead(s) below it in place. Take needle back through all except Stop Bead and through fabric. Pull thread snug to remove slack before proceeding to next bead.

Side view

Lazy Stitch

Bring needle up through fabric (A), pick up several seed beads, and go back through fabric near last bead on thread at B. At back of fabric move needle to next position (C) and repeat.

Side view

Bead-Sequin Stack

Bring needle up through fabric, pick up sequin and seed bead, and go back through sequin to back of fabric. Pull thread to take out slack.

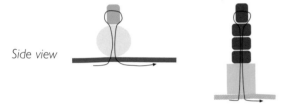

Side view

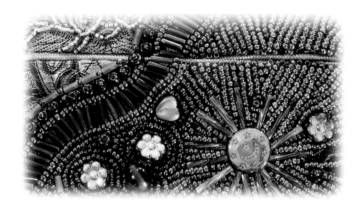

Criss-Crossed Strands on Buttons

You need a 4-hole button to make this work!
Bring needle up through the fabric and one hole in the button. Pick up several seed beads and go back through the hole in the button that is opposite/across, then through the fabric. At the back of the fabric, move the needle to come up through one of the open holes in the button. Pick up one or two more beads than you used to make the first stitch. Take the needle through the last open hole in button to the back of the fabric. Knot off.

Birds eye view

Lazy Stitch, Dimensional

Also called a Bead Bridge.
Bring up needle through fabric, pick up several seed beads and go back through fabric making a stitch shorter than the length of the beads, causing the beads to arch above surface of fabric. At back of fabric move needle to next position and repeat.

Side view

Lazy Daisy

Bring needle up at A. Pick up an even number of beads and go back through first bead and down at B close to A. Come up at C, take needle through one bead and go back down at D.

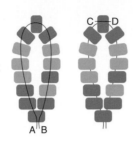

Birds eye view

Loops

This is like a lazy daisy stitch, except the loops are not tacked down.
Bring up needle through fabric at A, and pick up several beads. Take the needle back through the first bead and through fabric at B, forming a loop of beads. At back of fabric move needle to next position and repeat for next stitch.

Birds eye view

Chain Stitch

This stitch allows you to create a double row of beads.
Bring needle up at A. Pick up 4 or 6 (an even number of) beads and go back at B close to A. Bring needle up at C inside bead loop. Pick up an even number of beads and go back at D inside bead loop. Repeat. When slack is removed from thread the beads will lie close together and look like two continuous rows of beads.

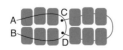

Birds eye view

Couch Beads (Around a Focal Bead)

Bring needle up through fabric next to focal bead (already stitched in place) and pick up enough seeds to encircle the bead. Take needle back through fabric (if you wish, you can go through a few of the first beads on the ring before going into fabric. Bring the needle up at A just outside the ring of beads you've stitched. Take needle across the thread forming the ring and down inside the ring. Repeat stitch at several points around bead ring.

Birds eye view

Couch with Beads

Use this technique to attach cords, fibers or yarn strands to fabric.
Bring the needle up at A next to cord. Pick up enough beads to span cord. Take needle across cord and back into fabric at opposite side.

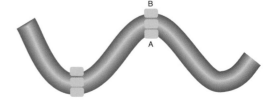

Birds eye view

Bead Ring

Bring up thread from back of fabric at A and pick up 12 seed beads. Take needle back through all beads in the same direction, snug beads to form a loop, and take needle into fabric at B. Bring needle back out near ring to couch in two or three places, shaping the ring as you do so.

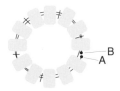

Birds eye view

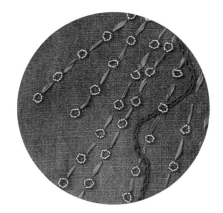

Picot Edging

Anchor stitch at edge of fabric. Pick up five seed beads (here, 2 cranberry, 1 gold, and 2 cranberry). Take stitch next to first stitch, allowing cranberry beads to touch and forcing the gold bead to stand out from edge a bit. Bring needle back out through last bead stitched and pick up 3 beads (here, 1 gold and 2 cranberry). Continue, adding 3 beads with each new stitch.

Side view

Three-Bead Clusters

Method #1: Bring up needle through fabric at A. Pick up 3 beads and take needle down at B. Come back up at C and go down through D, snugging the beads as close together as possible.

Birds eye view

A B   C D

Method #2: Bring up the needle at A, pick up 2 beads, and go down at B. Come back up between the beads at C, and take the needle across the thread in the previous stitch. Pick up a 3rd bead and go back down at D, keeping beads as close together as possible.

Birds eye view   A B

Embroidery Stitches

Blanket Stitch

Bring up needle at A, take back down at B, and bring back up at C, keeping thread under the point of the needle. Pull thread snug to form stitch.

Start next stitch by taking needle down at D, up at E. Repeat for each stitch.

End by coming up at D as usual, cross over, and take back down right next to thread at bend.

For a wavy blanket stitch, work in a rippling design instead of a straight row. Draw a line to follow with an air-erase fabric marker, if you wish.

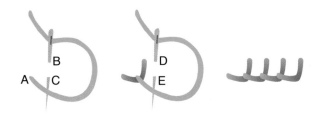

For a staggered blanket stitch, make the distance from B-C and D-E different lengths. In the example shown, three lengths were used. Stitch 2 is longer than 1, 3 is longer than 2. Stitch 4 is shorter than 3 (and same as stitch 2); stitch 5 is same length as stitch 1.

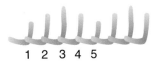

For short/long blanket stitches, alternate lengths of every other stitch.

Fly Stitch

Bring up needle at A, take back down at B, and bring back up at C, keeping thread under the point of the needle. Go back down at D. Pull thread snug to form stitch.

Variations: Make tail (distance from C to D) longer or shorter. Space stitches further apart or closer together.

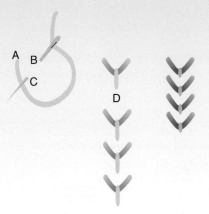

Fly Stitch, Side-by-Side

Make the fly stitch, working the stitches close together side-by-side with very short stems (C-D portion of stitch); the finished result will look like a row of zig-zag stitching.

Fly Stitch & Straight Stitch Combination

First part: Make fly stitch as above, up at A, down at B, up at C.
Second part: Make a straight stitch in center of fly stitch: come up at E and down at F.

Feather Stitch

Bring up needle at A, take back down at B, and bring up at C, keeping thread under the point of the needle. Move needle to left and make second stitch. Work a vertical row of alternating left and right stitches.

Variations: Work two or three stitches to right or left before changing directions.

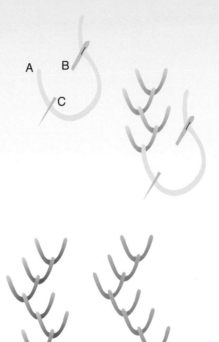

Herringbone Stitch

Bring up needle at A, take back down at B, and bring back up at C, left of B, to start next stitch. Work a horizontal row, left to right.

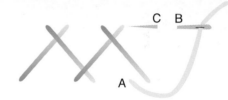

Split Stitch

Use size 5 or larger embroidery thread for best results.
Bring up needle at A, down at B, and back up at C, splitting the thread with each stitch.

Maidenhair Stitch

This is a variation of the Feather Stitch.
Bring up needle at A and take down at B. Come up at C, keeping the thread beneath the needle. Work a vertical row, making three graduated stitches to one side of the row, each slightly larger than the last and aligned vertically. Then work three stitches on the other side of the row.

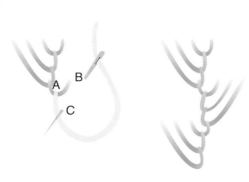

Lazy Daisy Stitch

Bring up needle at A. Go back down at B, right next to A. Come back up at C, keeping thread loop under needle. Pull up to make a small loop (not too tight). Take needle back down at D to hold the end of the loop in place against the fabric.

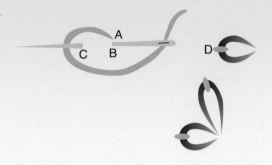

Chain Stitch

Bring up needle at A. Go back down at B right next to A to form a loop. Come back up at C, inside of loop. Take needle back down next to C inside of loop and come back up through second loop; repeat.

For a zig-zag chain stitch, change the angle of needle with each stitch.

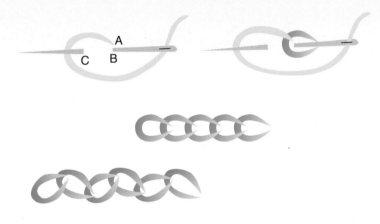

Cretan Stitch

Bring up needle at A, take back down at B, and bring up at C, keeping thread under the point of the needle. Change needle angle and go back down at D, come back up at E. Work from left to right.

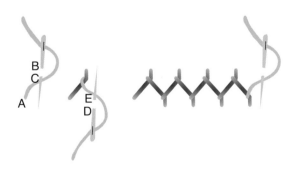

Running Stitch

This is as simple as 1-2!
Bring up needle at A and take it down at B. Keep going up and down, making a straight stitch each time. Vary the lengths of the stitches and the spaces between them for interest.

Inkjet Printing on Fabric

1. Place your chosen image(s) in a document that allows you to size and scale the image(s). Adjust the image size as needed to fit your chosen project surface. For this project, the image was sized to fit a 3-1/2" diameter circle. The 3-1/2" includes a 1/4" border so that, when framed, the image showing will be 3" in diameter.

2. Follow the fabric manufacturer's instructions for printing.

TIP: Economize by printing enough images at one time to fill a sheet or half sheet of inkjet-printable fabric. In the second example, half the sheet was printed and the sheet was carefully cut in half so the unprinted portion could be used for a later project.

Inkjet-printed fabric sheet.

Inkjet-printed fabric sheet, trimmed to one-half sheet.

Here are just a
few of the stitches you
will learn to make using
threads and beads!

(B) = Bead Stitch
(E) = Embroidery Stitch

Staggered Blanket (E)
Single - Seeds (B)

Single - Seeds (B)

Lazy Stitch, Dimensional (B)

Fly, Side-by-Side (E)
Lazy Daisy (E)
Single - Seeds (B)

Couch with Beads (B)

Single - Seeds (B)

Feather Stitch (E)
Single - Seeds (B)

Bead-Sequin Stack (B)

Bead Clusters (B)
Fly (E)
Single - Bugles (B)

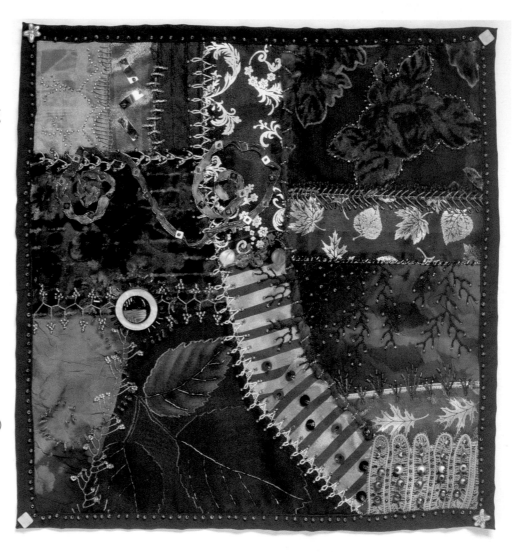

Cretan (E)
Single - Seeds (B)

Feather (E)
Single - Seeds (B)

Bead Stack (B)

Bead-Sequin Stack (B)

Fly-Straight Combination (E)
Single - Seeds and Bugles (B)

Backstitch (B)

Maidenhair (E)
Loops (B)

Bead Stack (B)

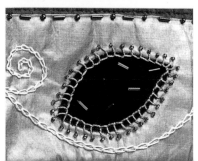

Beaded and Embroidered PROJECTS

Fashion as well as home décor accessories can look dazzling with some bead and embroidery embellishments. It's easy to add some sparkle and pizzazz to t-shirts, blouses, jeans, bags, home décor pillows, placemats and more. Almost everything shown here was purchased pre-made then embellishments added.

Gifting Bag

For a special-occasion gift, only a spectacular presentation will do. Here, six transfer images—three on each side—were applied to a gift bag and framed with beads and embroidery. One side of the bag is pictured, *right;* the other side is shown at the end of the project instructions. The vintage images convey your sentiments in a timeless way; substitute your own photos for an entirely different look.

Gift bag as purchased.

The threads.

The beads.

PROJECT SURFACE:
• Cloth gift bag, 7" × 12-1/2"

BEADS:
• Pearls, 2.5 mm to 3 mm
• Size 2 bugle beads - blue
• 3.5 mm color-lined cube beads - Lavender
• Size 11 seed beads - Pink, green, blue, purple, pale yellow, metallic gold

THREAD:
• Size 8 pearl cotton embroidery - Pink, blue, purple, hand-dyed variegated blue/purple/green
• 4 mm silk embroidery ribbon - Dark rose
• Blending filament for needlework - Gold
• Beading thread - Light, dark

TOOLS & OTHER SUPPLIES:
• 2 white buttons, 1/2" diameter
• Sharp scissors
• Beading needle
• Embroidery needle
• Computer and inkjet printer *or* other fabric image transfer method
• Inkjet-printable fabric
• Transfer images
• Fusible adhesive
• Paper

Stitches Used

See the "Stitching Basics" sections for instructions unless otherwise noted.

BEADING STITCHES:
• Single Stitch (seed and bugle)
• Lazy Daisy
• Bead Stack - *See Fig. A*

EMBROIDERY STITCHES:
• Blanket Stitch
• Long/Short Blanket Stitch
• Zig-Zag Chain Stitch
• Fly Stitch
• Fly and Straight Stitch Combination

Fig. A - Bead Stack - Side view

Take needle through one or more beads, ending with a seed bead to serve as the stop bead that holds the beads below it in place. Take the needle back through the beads and through the fabric. Pull thread snug to remove slack before proceeding.

Instructions

ATTACHING THE IMAGES:
See Inkjet Printing On Fabric technique on page 25.

1. Select and size six images—each should be about 2-1/2 x 3". Print on paper.

2. Trim and arrange on gift bag, three images per side.

3. When you are satisfied with the size and arrangement of the images, print them on inkjet-printable fabric. *(Photo 1)*

4. Remove the backing from the inkjet prints. Fuse adhesive to the back of the printed fabric sheet. Carefully trim images and remove paper liners. Fuse to gift bag. NOTE: Don't overlap images on the casing for the drawstring; stitching into the casing could compromise the functionality of the drawstring!

Photo 1 - Images printed on fabric.

EMBROIDERY:
One Side

1. Use variegated embroidery thread to blanket stitch around the first image on one side. *(Photo 2)*

2. Use purple pearl cotton to stitch a zig-zag chain around the second image. Accent this frame with a combination fly stitch and straight stitch worked in blending filament. *(Photo 3)*

3. Fly stitch with blue pearl cotton to frame the third image. *(Photo 3)*

Other Side

4. Use purple pearl cotton to stitch a zig-zag chain around one image. *(Photo 4)*

5. Use pink thread to work the short/long blanket stitch around another image. *(Photo 4)*

6. Single stitch pearls with silk embroidery ribbon around the remaining image. *(Photo 4)* Between each stitch, push the ribbon to make a gentle fold; occasionally add a twist as well. (This makes the frame softer and more appealing than simply stitching the ribbon flat.) Fold under the ribbon end to finish.

Photo 2 - Blanket stitching around first image.

Photo 3 - All images framed with embroidery on one side.

Photo 4 - Images framed with embroidery on other side.

BEADWORK ON FRAMES:
One Side

1. Single stitch a bugle bead between each blanket stitch and a Lazy Daisy at the end of each blanket stitch. *(Photos 5 through 10)*.

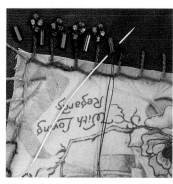

Photo 5 - Needle angle used to bead lazy daisy.

Photo 6 - Needle returning to fabric to make beaded lazy daisy.

Photo 7 - Aiming the stitch toward the end of the loop.

Photo 8 - Taking the stitch through the pink bead to tack down the loop.

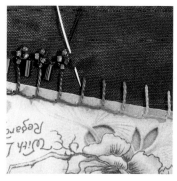

Photo 9 - Needle position to add the bugle bead between the blanket stitches.

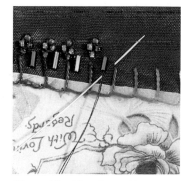

Photo 10 - Needle position to start next lazy daisy.

2. Single stitch a blue bead at each end of the fly stitches worked in blue thread. *(Photo 11)*

3. Single stitch a purple bead at each point of the zig-zag chain worked in purple thread. *(Photo 11)*

Photo 11 - Beading is complete on one side.

Other Side
4. Single stitch a pale yellow bead at the end of each blanket stitch worked in pink thread. *(Photo 12)*

5. Single stitch a purple bead at each point of the zig-zag chain worked in purple thread. *(Photo 12)*

ADDITIONAL BEADWORK:
1. Make a beaded fringe along the cuff edge by spacing bead stacks (See Fig. A) 1/2" apart all along the edge. Each stack consists of one cube, blue bugle, gold seed, blue bugle, and gold seed. *(Photo 13)*

2. Embellish the border around the bag below the panel with the images by alternating single-stitched cube beads with short bead stacks (one bugle bead and one gold seed bead), leaving 1/8" between each stitch. *(Photo 14)*

Photo 12 - Beading is complete on the other side.

Photo 13 - Bead fringe (made of bead stacks) around edge of cuff.

Photo 14 - The beaded border below the panel with the transferred images.

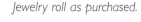

Jewelry roll as purchased.

Micro tube beads.

Beads for tassels.

Threads.

Jazzy Jewelry Roll

Silvery micro tube beads and metallic thread add a little bling to a flower-print fabric jewelry roll. A pattern for the scroll design appears on a following page.

Supplies

PROJECT SURFACE:
• Fabric jewelry roll

BEADS:
• 2 strands micro tube beads - Silver-lined clear
• Assorted seed beads, dagger beads, and small accent beads (for tassels)

THREAD:
• Blue beading thread (or color to complement your jewelry roll)
• Metallic multi-color sewing thread

TOOLS & OTHER SUPPLIES:
• Air-erase marker
• Small embroidery needle
• Beading needles, size 12, size 15

Stitches Used
See the "Stitching Basics" section for instructions.

BEADING STITCH:
• Backstitch

EMBROIDERY STITCHES:
• Running Stitch
• Feather Stitch

Photo 1 - A scroll drawn on the fabric with an air-erase marker.

Photo 2 - Working the beaded backstitch along the marked line.

Photo 3 - A second scroll drawn on the fabric.

Instructions

BEADING THE SCROLL DESIGN:

1. Using the pattern and the photos as guides, use the air-erase marker to draw a scroll shape on the cover of the jewelry roll. *(Photo 1)*

2. Work the beaded backstitch with micro tube beads along the scroll. *(Photo 2)* TIP: Working with such tiny beads can seem a bit daunting, but as long as you can see them and you have a needle small enough to easily pass through them, it's easy. If you have difficulty getting through the beads on the second pass, use a single strand of beading thread or switch to a lighter-bodied thread.

3. Draw a second scroll connecting to first scroll. *(Photo 3)*

4. Bring the thread out between two beads of the first scroll to begin beading second scroll. Continue beading the scroll. *(Photo 4)*

5. When you finish beading the second scroll, draw another scroll. *(Photo 5)*

6. Continue drawing and beading scrolls until you're pleased with the amount of beading. *(Photo 6)*

Pattern

Photo 4 - Backstitching the second scroll.

Photo 5 - Second scroll beaded, third is drawn.

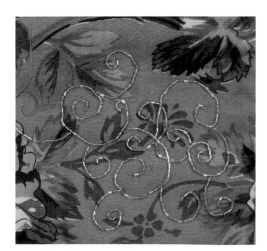

Photo 6 - Several scrolls are completed.

BEADED TASSELS:

1. Sew a running stitch along the ties of the jewelry roll, using metallic multi-colored thread and a small embroidery needle.

2. Switch to beading thread and a beading needle. Anchor the thread at the end of the tie. Pick up a large bead (it should have a hole large enough to accommodate many pass-throughs of thread) and several seed and rocaille beads, ending with a dagger bead. Go back through all but the dagger bead and stitch into the end of the tie. *(Photo 7)*

3. Bring the needle back through the large bead to start the second strand. *(Photo 8)*

4. Pick up seeds, rocailles, and a focal bead. End with a seed bead to act as a stop bead, then take needle back through all other beads in the strand, including the large bead next to the tie. *(Photo 8)*

5. Stitch into the tie, go back through the large bead, and begin the next strand. Make as many strands as you like.

6. Make a tassel at the end of the second tie.

EMBROIDERING THE BORDER:

There's no reason you couldn't make this step 1, if you like!

Feather stitch the entire border of the roll, using metallic multi-colored thread and a small embroidery needle.

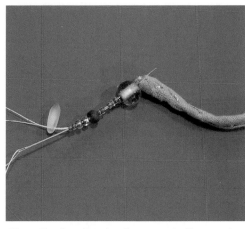

Photo 7 - Beading the first strand of a tassel.

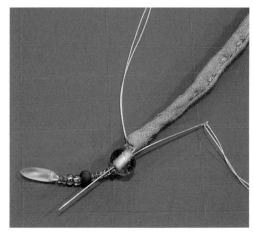

Photo 8 - Starting the second strand of the tassel.

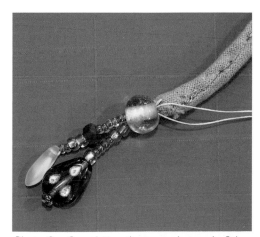

Photo 9 - Completing the second strand of the tassel.

Supplies

PROJECT SURFACE:
• Brown placemat quilted in a grid pattern

BEADS:
• Size 8 hex beads - Orange
• Size 11 seed beads - Gold
• Size 2 bugle beads - Bright gold
• Size 5 twisted bugles - Gold

THREAD:
• Beading thread - Brown

TOOLS:
• Beading needle

Stitches Used

See the "Stitching Basics" section for instructions.

BEADING STITCH:
• Single Stitch

Placemat Pizzazz

Use beads to add a bit of drama to a plain-Jane placemat; to make the stitches invisible, slide the needle along between the layers of fabric. TIP: Use doubled beading thread to withstand wear and laundering.

Instructions

BEADED DESIGN ALONG BOTH LONG EDGES:

1. Anchor the thread to a long edge of the placemat at one corner. Single stitch an orange hex bead to the edge where the stitching lines of the quilting meet. String on enough gold seeds to reach to the quilting intersection one square to the right. Make a small stitch into the fabric at the intersection.

2. Pick up three seeds, a hex, and one seed. Take the needle back through all but the last seed bead and back into the fabric at the same intersection.

3. Bring the needle back out at the same place and pick up the same number of seed beads you used in step 1. Stitch to edge of placemat at next quilted line.

4. Come back out and pick up an orange hex and seeds. Repeat the sequence along the entire long edge.

5. Work the other long edge of the placemat the same way.

BEADED FRINGE:

1. Anchor thread at outer corner of placemat. Pick up nine seed beads, one hex bead, and one seed bead. Go back through the hex bead and pick up nine seed beads. Stitch into the edge of the placemat at the quilting line.

2. Come back out through the last seed bead and pick up eight more seed beads, one hex bead, and one seed bead. Go back through hex bead and pick up nine seed beads. Stitch into the edge of the placemat at the next quilting line.

3. Repeat along all edges of the placemat, adjusting number of seed beads as necessary to make fringe even at the corners.

BEADED SHORT EDGES:

Stitch bugle beads to make borders along the two short edges of the placemat, placing one bead on each line of quilting.

ADDING SEED BEADS AT INTERSECTIONS:

Single stitch seed beads at outer three rows of quilting intersections as shown. Between each stitch, slide the needle between the layers of fabric to avoid having threads show on the back. *Option:* Cover entire placemat with seed beads at each intersection of the quilted lines. ◥◐◤

Supplies

PROJECT SURFACE:
- Quilted throw, 60" x 54"
- Sage silk, cut in strips 7" wide - two 56" long, two 62" long
- 1/2 yd. purple velveteen
- Heavy-weight fusible interfacing, cut in 3" strips, two 56" long, two 62" long
- 1/2 yd. fusible interfacing (in addition to the strips)

BEADS:
- 2 tablespoons size 8 seed beads - Purple
- 1 oz. size 2 bugle beads - Purple iris
- 2-3 tablespoons size 11 seed beads - Purple

Warm & Wonderful Throw

Customize a quilted throw with a dazzling border of embroidered and beaded velveteen appliques. I chose the colors for the border to coordinate with my purple throw. TIP: Use Japan-manufactured bugle beads for longer wear–their edges are less sharp than those of their Czech counterparts.

THREAD:
- Pearl cotton embroidery thread, size 8 - Pale mint green, purple
- Dark beading thread
- Sewing thread to match silk

TOOLS & OTHER SUPPLIES:
- Heavy card stock or cardboard (such as cereal box)
- Quick-dry fabric glue
- Scissors
- Sewing shears
- Straight pins
- Tracing paper
- Air-erase felt tip marker
- Beading needle
- Embroidery needle
- Sewing needle
- Iron and ironing board

Stitches Used

See the "Stitching Basics" section for instructions and diagrams.

EMBROIDERY STITCHES:

- Blanket Stitch
- Chain Stitch

BEADING STITCH:

- Single Stitch

Instructions

ASSEMBLING THE BORDER:

1. Fold silk strips in half lengthwise. Press to crease along folds.

2. Open up the strips. Position interfacing strips along one side of the fold in each strip, leaving 1/2" of silk at the edge without interfacing for turning under. Fuse.

3. Mark the center of each strip and the center of each side of the throw.

4. Align the folds of the longer strips with the longer edges of the throw and pin the strips to the throw to form the border. Fold under the ends of the strips so they are the same length as the throw.

5. Align the folds of the shorter strips with the shorter edges of the throw. Fold the corners at 45-degree angles. Press to mark.

6. Trim excess fabric for a smooth fit. Mark the lines of the mitered corners on the longer strips. Remove all the border strips from the quilt.

MAKING & ATTACHING THE APPLIQUES:

1. Fuse interfacing to wrong side of velveteen.

2. Trace pattern for leaf shape and transfer to card stock. Cut out to make template.

Pattern for leaf applique

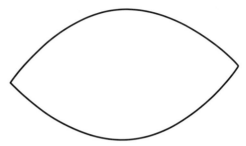

3. Trace around the leaf template on the back of the fused velveteen to make 52 appliques.

4. Cut out appliques.

5. Starting at the center of one border strip, place the velveteen leaves on the interfaced side of the silk strip. Use the pattern as a guide for placement and keep the leaves at least 1" from the cut edge of the silk strip. *Option:* Transfer the placement pattern for the border and use it as a guide. On shorter sides, place six leaves on each side of the center; on the longer sides, use seven leaves.

6. Working one at a time, lift each leaf and place a very small dab of glue on the back at the center. Re-position the leaves and allow them to dry (approximately 15 minutes). TIP: Use only enough glue to hold the leaves in place; too much glue will make it difficult to stitch through the leaves.

EMBROIDERY & BEADING:

1. Blanket stitch around each leaf with purple pearl cotton, making an extra stitch at each point.

2. Single stitch a size 11 seed bead at the end of each blanket stitch.

3. Sew a few bugle beads in the center of each leaf.

4. Using the placement pattern as a guide, draw the wavy lines on the silk strips, using the air-erase pen. TIP: You may need to redraw the lines if they disappear before you stitch over them.

5. Use the pale mint-green pearl cotton to chain stitch the wavy lines, then chain stitch the curlicues between the leaves.

ATTACHING THE BORDER:

1. Pin the longer strips to the throw.

2. Pin the shorter strips with the mitered corner folds in place.

3. Fold under 1/2" along the cut edges and pin securely.

4. To attach the strips to the throw quilt, anchor beading thread to the throw where the knot will be hidden by the border. Bring the thread up to the top of the throw and through the edge of the border strip. Pick up a size 8 bead and stitch in place through the silk border and the top layer of the throw. Slide needle ahead 1/8" and pick up a bugle bead; stitch in place, catching the silk border and the top layer of the throw.

5. Repeat all along the edges of the border, all around the throw. At the corners, stitch size 8 beads in same manner along the mitered folds.

6. Whip stitch the other edge of the border to the back of the throw, using sewing thread.

Placement Pattern for Border Enlarge 200% for actual size

Repeat as needed to right of center mark on each strip.

Repeat as needed to left of center mark on each strip.

Supplies

PROJECT SURFACE:
- Lavender velvet pillow with beaded fringe, 13" square

FABRICS FOR FLAP:
- Dark purple velveteen, 15" square
- Purple satin, 10" square
- Red-violet velvet, 9" square
- Dark purple lining, 15" square
- Purple lining, 10" square
- Red-violet lining, 9" square
- 1/2 yd. fusible interfacing

BEADS:
- Size 11 seed beads - Dark purple, medium purple, pale purple, green
- Size 10 seed beads - Purple-lined
- Size 8 seed beads - Lavender
- Size 8 hex beads - Deep magenta
- Size 10 square seed beads - Purple iris
- 4 mm square beads - Matte purple iris
- Size 3 bugle beads - Magenta
- 5/8" dagger beads - Purple
- 2 round 6 mm teal and purple beads
- 2 disc beads, 1/2"

THREAD:
- Size 8 pearl cotton embroidery thread - Purple
- Size 8 fine braid metallic - Green
- Beading thread -Purple
- Sewing thread - Purple

TOOLS & OTHER SUPPLIES:
- Sewing shears
- Embroidery needle
- Beading needle
- Straight pins
- Iron and ironing board
- Sewing needle
- *Optional:* Sewing machine

The pillow as purchased.

Photo 1 - Interfacing fused to wrong side of red-violet velvet.

Raspberry Dotted Pillow

A beaded triangular flap adds drama to a beautiful (but rather bland) velvet pillow. The pillow I used came with beaded fringe, but you could add your own fringe to a plain pillow.

Stitches Used
See the "Stitching Basics" section for instructions and diagrams.

EMBROIDERY STITCH:
- Chain Stitch

BEADING STITCHES:
- Single Stitch

Instructions for the other stitches used to make the raspberries are included with the instructions that follow.

Instructions

CUTTING THE PANELS:
1. Enlarge pattern as noted or to fit your pillow.

2. Using the pattern, cut interfacing.

3. Fuse interfacing to wrong side of red-violet velvet (panel 1 fabric). *(Photo 1)*

4. Using the pattern, cut three triangular panels (each includes 1/2" seam allowance):
   Panel 1 - red-violet velvet
   Panel 2 - purple satin
   Panel 3 - purple velveteen

5. Cut corresponding linings for each panel.

BEADED BERRIES:

Sew six beaded berries randomly over panel 1, keeping all stitching within interfaced area.

1. Using doubled beading thread and a needle, come up at A, pick up two size 11 beads, and take needle back into fabric at B to create the berry center. (Fig. A)

2. Bring needle back out through fabric near one of the beads at C. Pick up 10 beads and slide to fabric. Take needle back through all beads, beginning with first one strung. Gently pull up the slack in the thread so beads begin to form a ring. Pull thread snug, but not overly tight, forming a ring around center beads. Take needle down through fabric at D. (Fig. B)

3. Couch ring to fabric at three or four places. (Fig. C)

4. Bring needle back up through fabric in center of bead ring at E. Pick up a single bead and take needle back down at F, letting the new bead sit right on top of the original beads. (Fig. D)

5. Bring needle back up through fabric between ring and center beads. Pick up seven more beads and slide to berry. Take needle back through several beads strung in this step and gently pull up slack to form a second bead ring around the single bead added in step 4. (This new ring rests on top of the first ring.) (Fig. E)

6. Snug the ring and take the needle back into the fabric between the second ring and the first ring. Carefully couch to fabric in one or two places, hiding the stitches between the first ring and the berry center.

Fig. A

Fig. B

Fig. C

Fig. D

Fig. E

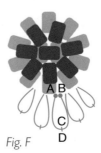

Fig. F

BRACTS & STEMS:

Use fine metallic green braid to stitch five lazy daisy stitches at the base of each berry and the tiny stems. Make the center stitch first and the two on each side of it slightly smaller.

1. Bring the needle up at A. Go back down at B, right next to A. Come back up at C, keeping thread loop under needle. Pull up to make a small loop (not too tight). Take needle back down at D to hold end of loop in place against fabric. (Fig. F)

2. Stitch a tiny stem using two or three split stitches below the bracts of each berry. Bring needle up at A, down at B, and back up at C, splitting the thread with each stitch. (Fig. G)

Fig. G

ASSEMBLING THE PANELS:

1. With right sides together, hand- or machine-sew lining to panel 1, leaving a 3" opening at one side for turning. Turn. Trim excess fabric at corners. Turn right side out and stitch opening.

2. With right sides together, hand- or machine-sew lining to panel 2, leaving a 3" opening at one side for turning. Turn. Trim excess fabric at corners. Turn right side out and stitch opening.

3. Center panel 1 on panel 2 and pin.

Photo 2 - Panel 1 attached to panel 2.

Photo 3 - The beaded tassel.

BORDER OF PANEL 1:

1. Anchor beading thread at back of panel 2 and take beading needle up through all layers, catching the edge of panel 1.

2. Pick up nine pale purple size 11 seed beads and slide to end of thread. Take the needle through the edge of panel 1, catching the satin layer of panel 2 approximately 1/2'' from where you came up. Go back through last bead stitched, pick up eight more beads. Catch the edge of panel 1 while attaching it to panel 2.

3. Repeat to finish the border on all sides of the panel.
(Photo 2)

EDGE OF PANEL 2:

1. Anchor thread at back near edge at top right corner. Pick up a bugle bead and take needle back into fabric at end of bugle.

2. Move needle slightly to the right, bring back out of fabric, and pick up a 4 mm square bead, five size 10 square beads, one size 8 lavender seed bead, and another size 10 square bead. Go back through all the beads but the last one, and go back into the fabric with the needle. Pull up slack in the stack of beads, move needle slightly to right and come back out of fabric. Pick up a bugle.

3. Repeat step 2.

4. Alternate bugle beads and bead stacks along the edge of the panel. As you reach the bottom point, adjust stitch lengths to end up with a stack just before the corner, a stack at the corner, and a stack just after the corner. Proceed as before, alternating bugles and stacks, and adjust the stitch lengths to place a stack at the other top corner of the panel as you work around.

TASSEL AT THE BOTTOM OF PANEL 2:

1. Anchor a new thread at the back of panel 2 at the bottom point. Bring out the thread through the 4 mm square bead of the bead stack at the bottom of the point. Pick up seven size 10 square seed beads, one size 8 lavender, one size 10 square, one size 8 lavender, 3 medium purple size 11 seeds, and one dagger. Reverse the order to complete the tassel, taking the needle and thread back through the 4 mm square.

2. Anchor the thread at the back of the fabric. Bring the needle back out through the 4 mm square bead of one of the side stacks at the point. Pick up the following beads: 3 size 10 square seeds, one size 8 lavender, one size 10 square, one size 8 lavender, eight size 10 squares, one 8 lavender, three size 10 squares, and a dagger. Reverse the sequence to complete the loop and take needle back into the 4 mm square bead at the other side of the tip. Anchor thread at back of fabric and trim. *(Photo 3)*

PANEL 3:

1. Trace the vine border pattern and cut out a template from interfacing.

2. Chain stitch the vine border around the perimeter of panel 3, using purple embroidery thread. There are two options:

Option 1 - Trace around the template on the interfacing on the wrong side of panel 3. (Photo 4) As you chain stitch the border, refer frequently to the traced lines on the wrong side of the panel.

Option 2 - Pin the template to the front of the panel and chain-stitch around the edge. Flip the template to stitch the second half (Photo 5)

3. Single stitch a dark purple seed bead in each chain-stitched loop. (Photo 6)

4. With right sides together, hand- or machine-sew lining to panel 3, leaving a 3" opening at one side for turning. Turn. Trim excess fabric at corners. Turn right side out and stitch opening.

5. Anchor thread at the back of panel 3 near the top left corner. Bring out of fabric at edge and pick up seven size 11 medium purple seed beads, one size 11 green seed bead, one size 8 hex bead, and one medium purple bead. Go back through the hex and green seed beads. Pick up seven more medium purple seed beads, and take a stitch into the fabric edge approximately 1/2" to right of where you started.

6. Take the needle back through the last bead stitched, and pick up six more purple seed beads.

7. Repeat the sequence to create a netted bead edging around the entire panel. At the top corners, make a small loop consisting of the same beads as a netted section, but take needle back into same bead instead of 1/2" away. (Photo 7)

8. At the bottom tip of the panel, stitch three dangling fringes, each with a hex bead, then seven purple seeds, a dagger, and two seeds. Then go back through the rest of the beads. Stitch into the fabric and move the needle slightly to start the next. Repeat for the third.

ASSEMBLY:

1. Center panel 3 on panel 2. Anchor thread at back of panel 3 and bring up through all layers in the upper corner of panel 2. Pick up a 6 mm round bead and a purple seed. Go back through the round bead and through all layers of fabric. Come back up through fabric, the layers, and the bead stack once more to secure. Knot off at back of fabric.

2. Repeat at other corner to attach panels 2 and 3.

3. Unzip the pillow cover or open one seam enough for access. Hand-stitch the panels to the pillow at the top corners.

4. Cover the stitches with disc beads. Make a small stitch to attach the panels at top center, catching only the lining of the panel. Close the pillow. ⚬⚬

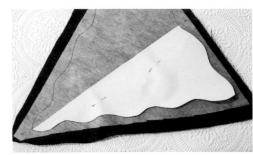

Photo 4 - **Option 1** - The vine border is traced on the wrong side of panel 3, using a template.

Photo 5 - **Option 2** - The border template is pinned to the front of panel 3 as a guide for the chain stitching.

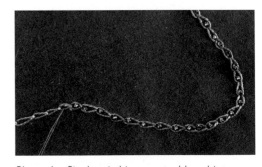

Photo 6 - Single stitching a seed bead into each chain stitch.

Photo 7 - The top corner of the pillow.

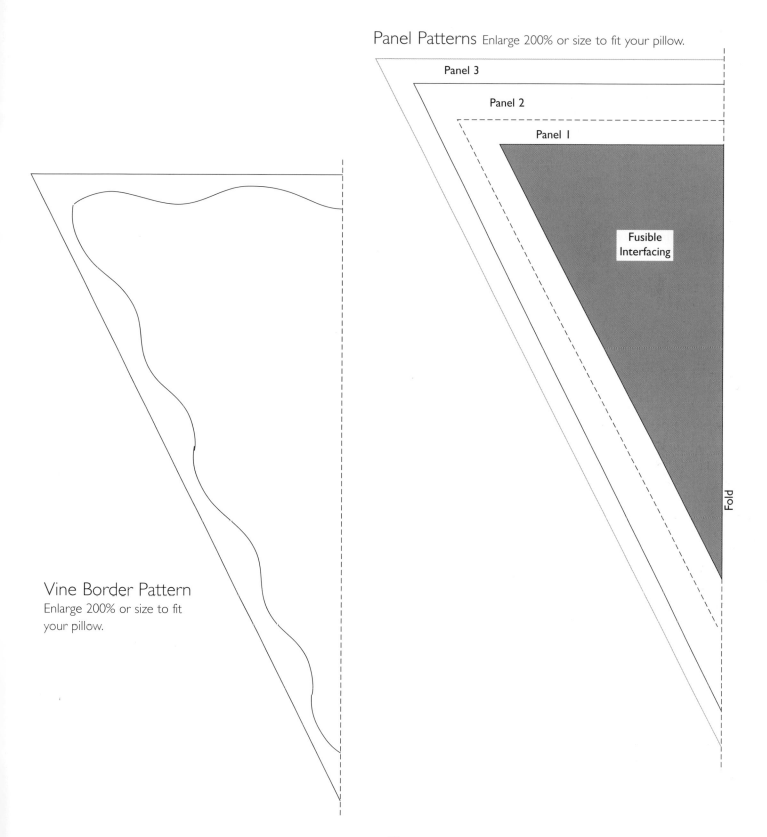

Panel Patterns Enlarge 200% or size to fit your pillow.

Panel 3

Panel 2

Panel 1

Fusible
Interfacing

Fold

Vine Border Pattern
Enlarge 200% or size to fit
your pillow.

Supplies

PROJECT SURFACE:
• Purchased fabric frame with 3" × 5" opening and lace embellishment

BEADS:
• Bead mix - Size 11 seed beads and small bugle beads in assorted colors *(Photo 1)*

THREAD:
• Beading thread - Light colored (or color to complement frame)

TOOLS & OTHER SUPPLIES:
• Beading needle
• Scissors

Stitches Used

See the "Stitching Basics" section for instructions unless otherwise noted.

BEADING STITCHES:
• Backstitch (Using bugles and seeds)
• Single Stitch (Bugles)
• Connected Bead Bridges - *See Fig. A.*
• Single Stitch (Seed Beads)

Instructions

1. Work a row of beaded backstitch all around the frame, about 1/2" from the opening, alternating short bugles and seed beads from your bead mix. *(Photo 2)*

2. Using bugle beads from your bead mix *(Photo 1)*, single stitch bugles around the frame opening. *(Photo 2)*

3. Work connected six-bead bridges (Fig. A) between the other rows of beadwork, alternating colors for the bridges and adjusting to end/begin bridges at corners.

4. Single stitch seed beads to the lace embellishment.

Door Sign with Style

A simple fabric frame can be easily dressed up with a few strategically placed beads. Use it to frame a sign or favorite photo.

Fig. A - Connected Bead Bridges - Side view
Bring up needle at corner of row and pick up seven beads. Take needle back into fabric, making a stitch shorter than length of beads and causing the beads to arch above surface of fabric.

Bring up needle through last bead stitched. Pick up six beads and go through fabric to back. Come back out through last bead stitched and repeat, adding six beads with each new stitch.

Photo 1 - The bead mix. You can buy beads already mixed or create a mix of your own.

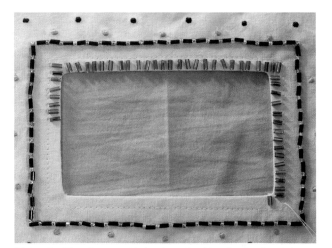

Photo 2 - The frame with backstitched bugles and seeds in place and bugle beads being single-stitched around frame opening.

Ribbon Wrapped Bolster

The colors of the bolster cover set the palette for the ribbons, threads, and beads. If the ribbons you want to use have wired edges, carefully pull the wires out of the casings before beading. (Needlenose pliers can help with this.) Work each ribbon, then attach to the bolster.

Stitches Used
See the "Stitching Basics" section for instructions.

EMBROIDERY STITCHES:
- Staggered Blanket Stitch
- Fly-Straight Stitch Combination
- Side-by-Side Fly Stitch
- Triple Feather Stitch

BEADING STITCHES:
- Single Stitch
- Lazy Daisy
- Bead Stack

Supplies

PROJECT SURFACE:
• Bolster pillow, 18" long, 6-1/2" diameter

RIBBONS:
• 5 ribbons, 1-1/2" to 2" wide, each 24" long, in colors to complement bolster fabric

BEADS:
• Size 11 seed beads - Green, metallic orange triangles, iris-finish black/green
• 3 strands size 11 seed beads - Silver-lined pink
• Size 15 seed beads - Green
• Size 8 seed beads - Green, orange, copper-lined clear
• Bugle beads - Mauve, iris-finish black/green
• Short bugle beads - Olive green
• 8 mm bicone beads - Gold

THREAD:
• Size 8 pearl cotton embroidery - Green, orange
• Hand-dyed embroidery thread - Variegated purple/green
• Size 8 metallic fine braid - Green
• Beading thread - Dark

TOOLS & OTHER SUPPLIES:
• Fusible interfacing
• Sewing shears
• Straight pins
• Embroidery needle
• Beading needle

Supplies for second ribbon: green bugles, green pearl cotton, hand-dyed embroidery thread, orange triangle beads and seed beads.

Bolster pillow as purchased.

Supplies for first and fourth ribbons: iris finish bugles; green seeds, sizes 8 and 15; orange pearl cotton; copper-lined size 8 seeds, mauve bugles.

Supplies for third and fifth ribbons: iris size 11 seeds, 8 mm gold bicones, metallic size 8 braid, size 8 orange beads, size 11 pink seeds.

Instructions

Ribbons are numbered in the instructions according to the order in which they appear, left to right, in the project photo. Ribbons can be worked in any order you like.

PREPARING RIBBONS FOR BEADING:

Cut strips of interfacing and fuse to wrong sides of ribbons. *(Photo 1)* TIP: This is a good way to use small leftover pieces of interfacing.

RIBBON #1:

1. Make a fly stitch at the center of ribbon as shown. *(Photo 2)* Make second fly stitch next to first one. *(Photo 3)* Work a row of side-by-side fly stitches along the center of the ribbon, creating a zig-zag effect. *(Photo 4)*

2. Single stitch a mauve bugle bead at each point along the fly stitching. *(Photo 5)*

3. Single stitch a size 8 clear copper-lined bead between each bugle bead. *(Photo 5)*

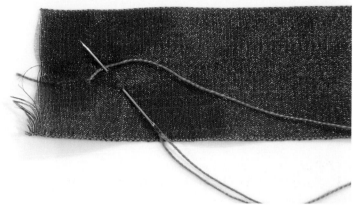

Photo 2 - Ribbon #1, begin fly stitching.

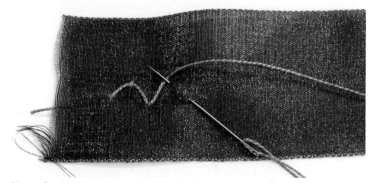

Photo 3 - Making the second fly stitch.

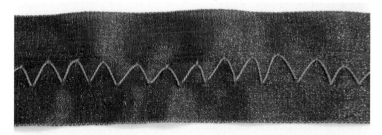

Photo 4 - A row of side-by-side fly stitches.

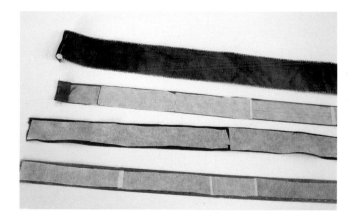

Photo 1 - Interfacing fused to wrong side of ribbons.

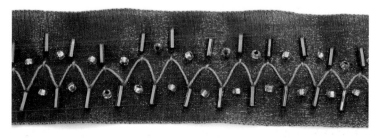

Photo 5 - Beads added to first ribbon.

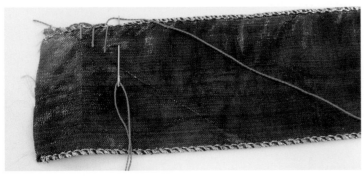

Photo 6 - Starting the blanket stitching on one edge of Ribbon #2.

Photo 7 - Blanket stitching on one edge.

Photo 8 - Making flowers with the fly stitch and straight stitch combination.

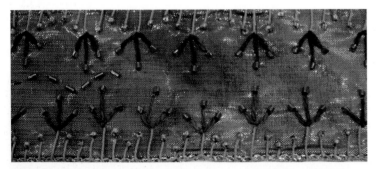

Photo 9 - Orange beads are added to the end of each flower stitch. Green seed beads are stitched at the end of each short blanket stitch. Short green bugles single stitched in a zig-zag down the center.

RIBBON #2:

This is the widest ribbon.

1. With green pearl thread, work a staggered blanket stitch along both edges. *(Photo 6, Photo 7)*

2. Work combination fly and straight stitch motifs at the ends of the longest blanket stitches, using variegated embroidery thread. *(Photo 8)*

3. Single stitch one size 11 orange triangle at end of each fly/straight stitch. *(Photo 9)*

4. Single stitch a size 11 green bead at end of each short blanket stitch. *(Photo 9)*

5. Stitch short green bugles in zig-zag pattern down center of ribbon. *(Photo 9)*

RIBBON #3:

Since this ribbon is already heavily embroidered, I simply added bead stacks consisting of one 8 mm gold bead held in place with a size 11 iris-finish green/black bead. The bead stacks are spaced 1" apart along the intersections of the embroidery on the ribbon.

RIBBON #4:

1. Single stitch iris-finish green/black bugles alternated with size 8 green beads along each edge of the ribbon. *(Photo 10)*

2. Following the woven pattern in the ribbon, single stitch size 15 green beads to outline the pattern. *(Photo 10, Photo 11)*

RIBBON #5:

1. With metallic fine braid, embroider triple feather stitch down the center of the ribbon. *(Photo 12)*

2. At end of each feather stitch, bead a lazy daisy using one size 8 orange bead at the base and 12 to 13 size 11 pink beads. *(Photo 13)*

Photo 10 - Ribbon #4 with beading along both edges and stippling begun.

Photo 11 - Bead stippling following the pattern in the ribbon.

Photo 12 - Fly stitching down the center of Ribbon #5.

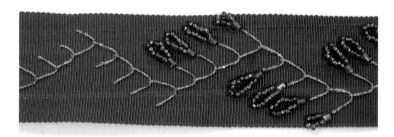

Photo 13 - Lazy daisy beadwork added to fly stitching.

ASSEMBLY:

1. Unzip bolster cover. (Photo 14)

2. Determine how you want to arrange the ribbons and pin them to the pillow cover.

3. Fold under the ends of the ribbons along the zipper opening and whipstitch each ribbon end to the pillow cover. (Photo 15)

If your pillow cover doesn't have a zipper, overlap the ribbon ends and fold the topmost ribbon under for a finished edge. Whipstitch each ribbon together at ends, then tack to the pillow cover along the seam of the cover.

Photo 14 - The bolster unzipped.

Photo 15 - Stitching ribbons to the pillow cover along the zipper opening.

Supplies

PROJECT SURFACES:
- 1 rectangular Battenburg doily, 6" x 10"
- 1 round Battenburg doily, 6" diameter with 2-3/4" center

BEADS & BUTTONS:
- Size 11 seed beads - Opaque pale yellow, pearl white
- 12 pale yellow pearls, 8 mm
- 8 white 2-hole buttons, 3/4" diameter
- 2 white 4-hole buttons, 1/2" diameter

THREAD:
- Size 8 pearl cotton embroidery - Pale yellow
- Beading thread - White

TOOLS & OTHER SUPPLIES:
- 1 yd. pale yellow ribbon, 1/2" wide
- Computer and inkjet printer (or other fabric image transfer method)
- Inkjet-printable fabric
- Transfer image
- Lightweight cardboard, 5" x 7"
- Glue gun and glue sticks
- Sewing shears
- Straight pins
- Beading needle

Framed in Lace

Layers of lace, pearly beads, and buttons create a frame to surround a precious image. The motifs within the lace provide obvious places to add buttons and pearl embellishments.

Wouldn't this be a sweet nursery decoration to welcome a newborn?

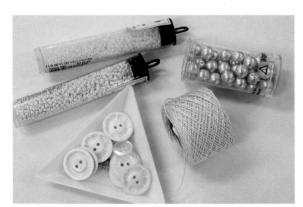

The beads, thread, buttons, and pearls.

Two Battenburg doilies.

Stitches Used

See the "Stitching Basics" section for instructions.

EMBROIDERY STITCH:
• Blanket Stitch

BEADING STITCHES:
• Single Stitch (seed beads)
• Button & Bead Stack - *See Fig. A*
• Criss-Crossed Strands

Instructions

POSITIONING THE IMAGE:
*See Inkjet Printing On Fabric technique
on page 25.*

1. Size and print image to fit in center of round battenburg doily.

2. Use sharp fabric shears to carefully trim the image, leaving a 1/2" border. *(Photo 1)*

3. Remove the center of the round battenburg doily. *(Photo 1)*

4. Place the image at the center of the rectangular doily. Place the round doily over the image to frame the image.
(Photo 2)

EMBROIDERY & BEADING:
1. Blanket stitch with pale yellow pearl cotton around the image, stitching through all layers of fabric. *(Photo 3)*

2. Single stitch one pale yellow seed bead at the end of each blanket stitch around the opening in the doily. *(Photo 4)*

3. Single stitch a pearl white seed bead between each blanket stitch. *(Photo 4)*

Photo 1 - The doily with the center removed; the image trimmed to fit the opening in the doily.

Photo 2 - Doilies stacked with the image pinned in place.

Photo 3 - Blanket stitching around the image.

Photo 4 - Adding seed beads and button-bead stacks.

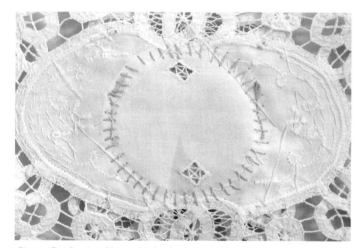

Photo 5 - Back of large doily showing oval shape.

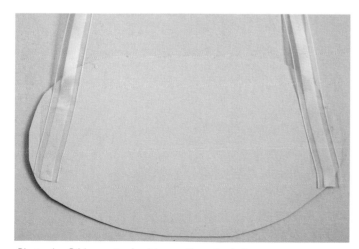

Photo 6 - Ribbon attached to cardboard reinforcement.

4. Single stitch white seed beads to all wide portions of the doilies and use them to stipple any solid areas of fabric. Do not stitch through multiple layers of fabric; leave the smaller doily unattached to the large one except at the center where it frames the image. *(Photo 4)*

5. Stitch four button-pearl-white seed bead stacks (Fig. A) at each corner of the small doily, going through all layers. *(Photo 4)*

6. Single-stitch four pearls at 12 o'clock, 3 o'clock, 6 o'clock, and 9 o'clock positions between the button stacks.

7. Stitch four button-pearl-white seed bead stacks (Fig. A) at each corner of the large doily.

8. Stitch smaller buttons at the center of each side, using criss-crossed strands of pale yellow seed beads.

FINISHING:
1. Cut out lightweight cardboard to fit the solid fabric area of the large doily. *(Photo 5)*

2. Position ribbon on cardboard and glue ends in place. *(Photo 6)*

3. Glue cardboard to back of doily, sandwiching ribbon ends between doily and cardboard.

4. Cut ribbon at center and tie into a bow for a pretty hanger. ❀

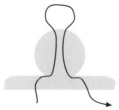

Fig. A - *Button & Bead Stack - Side view*

A two-hole button works best!

Bring up needle through fabric and one hole of button. Pick up pearl and seed bead. Go back through pearl and through other hole in button to back of fabric. Pull thread to take out slack. Make an anchor stitch or knot off at back of fabric.

Beads & Batik Pillow

Even a "busy" fabric can be improved by the addition of beadwork—the trick is to complement rather than compete with the existing pattern. For a final touch, a fabric-covered button was beaded and attached at the center of the pillow. Patterns for the beading template and the button decoration appear on page 65.

Supplies

PROJECT SURFACE:
• Decorative pillow, 18" square

BEADS:
• 5 strands size 11 seed beads - Dark blue
• 4 strands size 11 seed beads - Matte finish light blue
• Size 6 rocailles - Light blue
• Size 11 hex seed beads - Light blue
• 1 faceted bead, 4 mm - Medium blue

THREAD:
• Beading thread - Dark
• Heavy duty thread

TOOLS & OTHER SUPPLIES:
• Straight pins
• 2-1/2" half ball button for covering
• Coordinating fabric (for covering button), 4" circle
• Fusible interfacing, 4" circle
• Fabric marker
• Beading needle
• Rug needle
• Tracing paper (for template)
• Scissors

Stitches Used
See the "Stitching Basics" section for instructions and diagrams.

BEADING STITCHES:
• Backstitch
• Bead Netting - *See Fig. A.*

Instructions

BEADING THE PILLOW:

1. Trace pattern and cut out to make template.

2. Pin to pillow at one corner. *(Photo 1)* The curved edge of the template will be your guide for stitching a bead row to the pillow fabric.

3. Anchor thread to pillow near center of template curve. Work six-bead backstitch using size 11 matte beads along the edge of the template toward the edge of the pillow. *(Photo 2)*

Seed beads.

Beads for netting.

Faceted beads for the button. (Only one is used.)

Photo 1 - The template is pinned to first corner.

Photo 2 - Start the beaded backstitch near the center of the template.

Photo 3 - Four curved rows of beaded backstitching completed.

Photo 4 - The 2-1/2" circle marked on interfacing side of button fabric and spiral pattern marked inside the circle.

4. When you reach the edge of the pillow, knot off the thread in the pillow seam. Anchor a new thread under the beaded row near the previous starting point. Work a six-bead backstitch row to the other edge of the pillow, again following the curve of the template.

5. Reposition the template at the opposite corner of the pillow. Repeat steps 3 and 4, again using 11 matte beads to make the backstitched bead rows.

6. Move the template to one of the remaining corners. Switch to 11 dark blue beads and stitch, repeating steps 3 and 4.

7. Move the template to the remaining corner and backstitch the curved row with dark blue beads. *(Photo 3)*

BEADING THE BUTTON:

1. Fuse interfacing to the wrong side of the coordinating fabric.

2. Trace the button pattern. Trace around the 3-3/4" circle pattern. Trim.

3. On the back (interfacing) side, center and transfer the 2-1/2" circle. *(Photo 4)*

4. Starting at the center, transfer or draw the spiral pattern inside the circle. *(Photo 4)*

5. Anchor the beading thread at the center of the spiral on the wrong side of the fabric circle and bring needle to front. Single stitch the 4 mm faceted bead at the center and send needle back through it.

6. Continue with the beaded backstitch, following the spiral design using size 11 matte beads. *(Photo 5)*

7. Cover the button, following the button manufacturer's instructions. *(Photo 6)*

Photo 5 - The faceted bead is stitched to the center. The beaded backstitch is started.

Photo 6 - Button components ready for assembly.

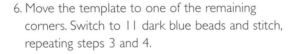

Fig. A - Bead Netting

Photo 7 - Bead netting started at the button edge.

8. Anchor beading thread at the edge of the covered button, hiding the knot on the back. To start the bead netting (Fig. A), pick up six matte seeds, a rocaille, a hex, and five or six dark blue seed beads. Take the needle back through the hex and rocaille. Pick up six matte seed beads and take the needle into the button edge, 1/4" to 3/8" from first leg. Pull up slack so beads are snug along the thread, then make a small stitch in fabric to secure. Bring needle back out through last seed. *(Photo 7)*

9. Pick up five more matte seeds, a rocaille, a hex, and five or six dark blue seed beads. Take the needle back through the hex and rocaille. Pick up six matte seed beads and take the needle into the button edge, 1/4" to 3/8" from the second leg to make the next netting section.

10. Work netting around button. For the second leg of the last section, pick up only five matte seeds, then take needle back through first bead in step 8 to join the netting. Anchor thread at back of button and trim.

SEWING THE BUTTON TO THE PILLOW:

1. Thread a rug needle with heavy-duty thread. Anchor at center back of pillow and take needle through to front of pillow. *(Photo 8)* Pull thread tightly and make a small stitch with the thread, emerging at the back of the pillow to make a dimple.

2. Make a second stitch at the back of the pillow to secure the dimple. Go back through to the front and stitch the button to the pillow front so it rests in the dimple. *(Photo 9)* TIP: It may be difficult to make several stitches and keep the button tight to the fabric. Make as many stitches as possible before knotting off at the back of the pillow. (Heavy-duty thread will hold the button securely with fewer stitches.) ✺

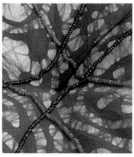

Photo 8 - To attach button, bring anchored thread up through the pillow at the center.

Photo 9 - The button stitched in place.

Pattern for Template
Enlarge 200% for actual size.

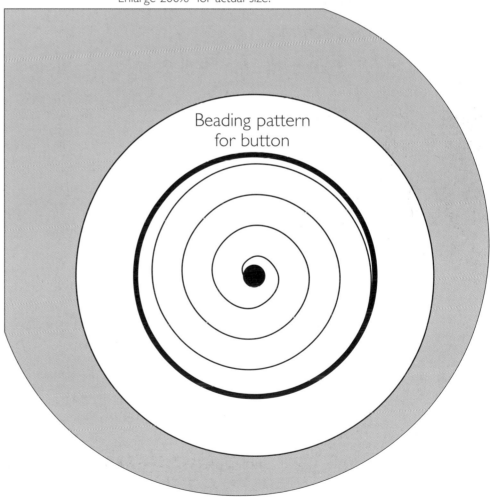

Beading pattern for button

Supplies

PROJECT SURFACE:
• Rounded square pillow with center button

BEADS:
• 5 strands size 11 seed beads - Silver-lined purple
• 2 strands size 8 seed beads - Copper-lined clear
• 12 flat oval beads - Purple
• 4 tri-cut beads, 8 mm - Purple and gold

THREAD:
• Beading thread - Dark

TOOLS & OTHER SUPPLIES:
• Air-erase fabric marker
• Ruler
• Short beading needle (for pillow)
• Long beading needle (for tassels)

The beads.

Graphic & Gorgeous Pillow

The unusual shape of this pillow inspired the design for the beadwork, but a round pillow would work as well if it were divided into quadrants and worked the same way. A few beads really made a striking decor piece out of a plain pillow.

Stitches Used
See the "Stitching Basics" section for instructions and diagrams.

BEADING STITCH:
• Backstitch

Instructions

BEADING TO THE CORNERS AND MAKING THE TASSELS:

1. Using a short beading needle, anchor the thread behind the button. *(Photo 1)*

2. Pick up six size 8 beads and slide them toward the button. *(Photo 2)*

3. Backstitch a row of beads to the corner of the pillow, adding six beads with each stitch. *(Photo 3)* TIP: To keep your row of beading straight, after picking up 6 new beads, align thread with corner (your end point). Follow this line as you stitch the beads in place.

4. At the end of the row, knot off the thread, hiding the knot in the pillow seam or beneath the row of beads.

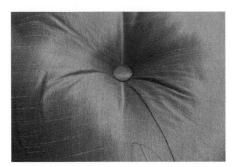

Photo 1 - Anchoring the thread behind the button.

Photo 2 - Sliding six beads on the thread toward the button.

Photo 3 - The first row of beads backstitched.

Photo 4 - The first loop of the tassel completed.

5. Using a long beading needle, anchor new thread at the end of the row. Pick up a tri-cut bead, 1-1/8" of size 11 seed beads, a size 8 bead, and 1-1/8" of size 11 seeds. Slide all the beads to the pillow and take the needle back through the tri-cut bead. Make a stitch into the pillow to secure. This completes the first (shortest) loop of the corner tassel. *(Photo 4)*

6. Bring the needle back out through the tri-cut bead. Pick up 2-1/8" of size 11 seeds, one size 8 seed bead, and 2-1/8" size 11 seed beads. Go back through the tri-cut bead and make stitch into the pillow to secure. This completes the second (longest) loop of the tassel. *(Photo 5)*

7. Bring the needle back out through the tri-cut bead. Pick up 1-3/4" of size 11 seeds, one size 8 seed bead, and 1-3/4" size 11 seed beads. Go back through the tri-cut bead and make a stitch into the pillow to secure. This completes the third loop of the tassel. *(Photo 6)*

8. Repeat steps 1 through 7 to complete the other three rows from the center to the corners and the corner tassels. *(Photo 7)* TIP: Rows can be smoothed or straightened by running the needle and thread back through the entire row.

Photo 5 - The second loop of the tassel added.

Photo 6 - The third loop of the tassel is completed.

Photo 7 - The four rows of beads to the corners and the tassels completed.

Photo 8 - Marked dots indicate the ends of the three beaded rows within a quadrant.

BEADING THE ROWS WITHIN THE QUADRANTS:

1. Use an air-erase marker to make a dot midway between two corners and 2" from the bottom of the pillow. Using the photo as a guide, make two more marks, one on either side of the first one. These marks are the end points for three rows of beads within that quadrant. *(Photo 8)*

2. Using a short beading needle, anchor the thread behind the center button. Align the needle with the middle dot to determine the line for the next row of beads. *(Photo 9)*

3. Backstitch a row of size 11 beads to the middle dot, adding six beads with each stitch. At the end of the row pick up an oval bead and a seed bead and stitch to pillow.

4. Slide the needle under the pillow fabric and bring out at another dot. Start the row with one size 11 seed, an oval bead, and two size 11 seed beads. Continue the row, backstitching toward the center button, adding six seed beads with each stitch. *(Photo 10)*

5. At the center button, anchor the thread and move the needle to start the third row in the quadrant. Stitch third row of size 11 seed beads, ending with an oval and a single seed, and anchor the thread behind the oval bead. Knot off and trim the thread close to the fabric. *(Photo 11)*

6. Repeat steps 1 through 4 in this section to complete the beaded rows in the remaining three quadrants. TIP: Align the thread often with the dots you marked to keep the rows straight. *(Photo 12)* 👓

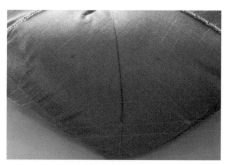

Photo 9 - Aligning the needle with a dot to determine the beading line.

Photo 11 - One quadrant completed; second section begun.

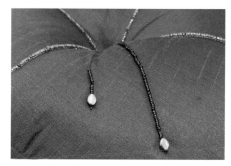

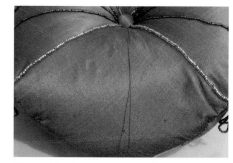

Photo 10 - One row completed; the second row begun.

Photo 12 - Lining up the thread with the marked dot helps keep rows straight.

Supplies

PROJECT SURFACE:
- Cocktail napkin, 6" square
- Round Battenburg doily, 4-3/4" diameter with 2" center

BEADS:
- Size 11 seed beads - Silver-lined red, opaque pearl white
- 2 size 5 or 6 rocaille beads - Red

THREAD:
- Beading thread - White, dark

TOOLS & OTHER SUPPLIES:
- 2/3 yd. variegated red crinkled ribbon, 1/4" wide
- Sewing shears
- Straight pins
- Beading needle
- Photo

Stitches Used

See the "Stitching Basics" section for instructions and diagrams.

BEADING STITCHES:
- Single Stitch (seed beads)
- Bead Stack
- Picot Edging - *See Fig. A*

Small & Lacy Frame

Stacked and layered fabric elements embellished with beadwork create a special keepsake frame for a favorite photo.

I started with a cocktail napkin embroidered with red dots, and chose red beads and red ribbon to complement the embroidery. A picot edging around the lace doily was created with beads.

Instructions

1. Use fabric shears to remove the center area of the Battenburg doily. *(Photo 1)*

2. Position doily "frame" on cocktail napkin. Pin in place.

3. Attach ribbon to doily with single-stitched red seed beads, stitching through all layers using dark beading thread. *(Photo 2)*

4. Fold the ribbon end under to overlap the beginning and stitch in place with a bead.

Cocktail napkin and small doily.

Beads and ribbon.

Photo 1 - Doily with center removed.

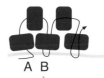

Fig. A - Picot Edging - Side view

Anchor the stitch at the back edge of the doily. Pick up three seed beads to start. Take a stitch in the edge of the doily next to the first stitch, allowing beads to touch and forcing the center bead to stand out from the edge a bit. Bring the needle back out through the last bead stitched and pick up two beads. Continue along edge of doily, adding two beads with each new stitch. At the end, take the needle back through the first bead stitched. Knot off at back of doily.

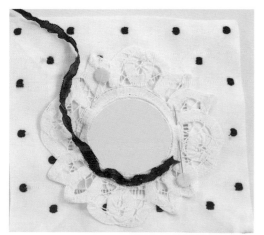

Photo 2 - Using seed beads to attach the ribbon.

5. Switch to white beading thread and picot stitch (Fig. A) red beads around the edge of the doily *only*—do not stitch the edge of the doily to the napkin.

6. Trim a photo slightly larger than the frame opening and insert it between the doily frame and napkin.

ATTACHING THE HANGER:

Use the remaining ribbon to form a hanger.

1. Stitch one end to each upper corner of the napkin, using a red rocaille and white seed bead stack.

2. Bring the needle back up through the fabric and ribbon next to the rocaille. String on enough red beads to completely encircle the rocaille. Couch across the ring in several places to secure.

Embellished Flower Placemat

I found this pretty placemat on a store shelf. Its embroidered flower and darker green border just begged for some beading.

Supplies

PROJECT SURFACE:
• Embroidered fabric placemat with border

BEADS:
• Size 1 bugle beads - Olive
• Size 15 seed beads - Light olive (olivine)
• 4 size 8 seed beads - Olive
• Size 11 seed beads - Red, dark pink
• 2 heat-set crystals, 6 mm (30 ss) - Dark yellow

THREAD:
• Beading thread - Dark

TOOLS & OTHER SUPPLIES:
• Beading needle
• Crystal heat-set tool

Stitches Used
See the "Stitching Basics" section for instructions unless otherwise noted.

BEADING STITCHES:
• Single Stitch
• Beaded Backstitch
• Bead Loops - *See Fig. A*
• Lazy Daisy

Placemat as purchased.

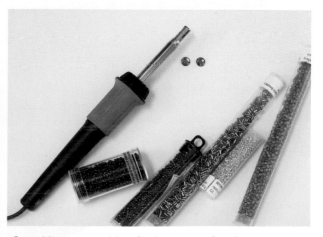

Crystal heat-set tool, hot fix rhinestones, beads.

Instructions

1. Single stitch bugle beads around the inside of the border, leaving about 1/16" between each bead. Leave gaps where embroidered leaves overlap frame. At each corner, single stitch a size 8 seed bead. *(Photo 1)*

2. Backstitch the stems and leaf veins, using six size 15 seed beads per stitch and following the lines in the embroidery. *(Photo 2)*

3. Heat-set a dark yellow rhinestone at the center of each flower. *(Photo 3)*

4. Stitch bead loops (Fig. A) over the outer petals of the large flower, using red seed beads (approximately 20 beads per loop). *(Photo 4)*

5. Stitch more bead loops over the inner petals, using dark pink seed beads (about 16 beads per loop). *(Photo 5)*

6. Add more dark pink bead loops around the center, using about 11 beads per loop. *(Photo 6)*

7. Stitch alternating red and pink lazy daisy beading stitches beadwork on the petals of the smaller flower. 👓

Fig. A - Bead Loop - Birds eye view

Bring the needle up at one side of the inner petal. Pick up the suggested number of seed beads. Take the needle back through the fabric at the opposite side of the inner petal, allowing the loop of beads to dangle freely. Move needle over a bit to start next petal. Repeat.

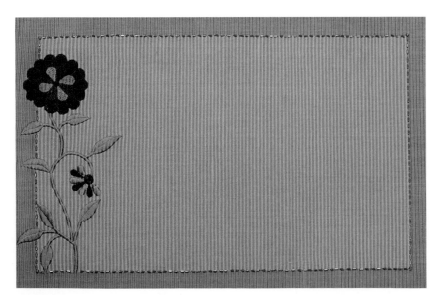

Photo 1 - Single stitched bugle beads around the inside of the placemat border.

Photo 2 - Backstitched bead stems and veins of leaves.

Photo 3 - Heat set rhinestones at flower centers.

Photo 5 - Bead loops stitched to inner petals.

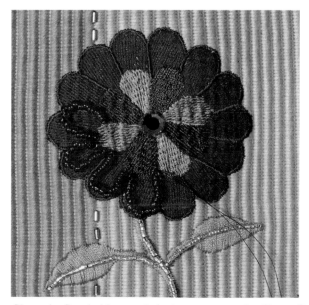

Photo 4 - Beaded loops stitched to outer petals of large flower.

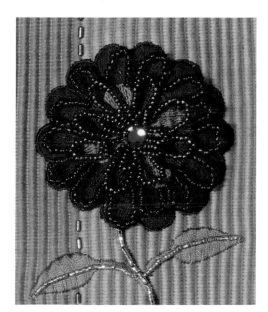

Photo 6 - Small bead loops stitched around center.

Memorable Memo Board

To make this memo board, start with a fabric you like and select ribbons and beads in colors to complement. Treat each ribbon as a separate work of art—you'll have a sampler of your skills to display and enjoy.

Ribbons may be worked in any order, using any combination of embroidery and beadwork. Instructions begin on page 78.

Stitches Used

See the Stitching Basics section for instructions.

EMBROIDERY STITCHES
- Cretan Stitch
- Maidenhair Stitch
- Split Stitch
- Herringbone Stitch
- Fly Stitch
- Feather Stitch
- Blanket Stitch

BEADING STITCHES
- Single Stitch
- Lazy Daisy Stitch
- Lazy Stitch
- Bead-Sequin Stack
- Couch
- Three-Bead Cluster

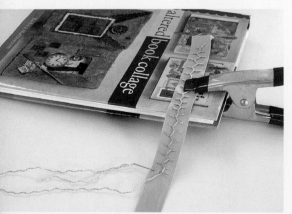

A Third Hand

Use a simple clamp to make a "third hand" to hold the ribbon while you work. You can devise a simple third hand using a clamp and book (shown in the photo) or clamp the ribbon to the edge of your work surface. A quilt clip is useful for keeping ribbon folded in half near your stitching; reposition it along ribbon length as you work. *(See Photo 16)*

Supplies

PROJECT SURFACE:
- Plastic foam (such as Styrofoam®) board, 1" x 12" x 36"
- Medium batting, 28" x 34"
- Fabric, 28" x 34"

RIBBONS & CORD:
- Ribbon, 1-1/2" wide (See Fig. A for lengths.) - Ombre green/orange/pink, sheer copper, sheer green (If using wire-edge ribbon, remove wires.) TIP: If you fold 1-1/2" wide ombre ribbons lengthwise, the ribbon will look different on each side, offering two color variations.
- Gold grosgrain ribbon, 1" wide (See Fig. A for lengths.)
- 2 yd. satin covered cord - Rust

BEADS & SEQUINS:
- Seed beads, size 8 and size 11 - Golds, greens, rust or copper, pinks, pink mix, oranges
- Bugle beads - Pink, orange, green
- Assorted leaf beads
- Square sequins - Gold

THREAD:
- Beading thread - Green, dark color
- Size 8 or 5 pearl cotton and hand-dyed embroidery thread - Gold, variegated greens, oranges

TOOLS & OTHER SUPPLIES:
- Gem glue
- Glue for plastic foam
- 1 yd. 18- or 20-gauge wire
- Sewing shears
- Straight pins
- Floral pins
- Needle tool
- Needlenose pliers
- Embroidery needle
- Beading needle
- Round toothpicks

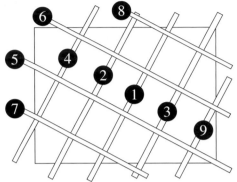

Lengths:
- Ribbon 1 (gold grosgrain) - 30"
- Ribbon 2 (green/orange ombre) - 30"
- Ribbon 3 (pink/orange ombre) - 28"
- Ribbon 4 (sheer green) - 25"
- Ribbon 5 (gold grosgrain) - 36"
- Ribbon 6 (sheer copper) - 30"
- Ribbon 7 (ombre) - 27"
- Ribbon 8 (sheer green) - 17"
- Ribbon 9 (sheer copper) - 19"

Fig. A - Ribbon placement diagram

Ribbons and fabric.

Leaf beads.

Beads and sequins.

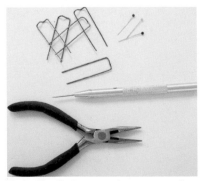

Tools: Floral pins, straight pins, needle tool, needlenose pliers.

Thread and cord.

Photo 1 - *Toothpicks inserted in one edge of foam to join panels.*

Photo 2 - *Foam panels are glued to make 18" x 24" board.*

Photo 3 - *Foam board placed face down on batting.*

Photo 4 - *Corners of batting clipped; batting wrapped.*

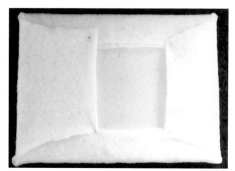

Photo 5 - *Batting pinned in place.*

Photo 6 - *Front of batting-wrapped memo board.*

Photo 7 - *Fabric wrapped around three sides of board; corners folded and pinned.*

Photo 8 - *Folding the fabric to miter corners.*

Instructions

COVERING THE BOARD:

1. Cut plastic foam board in half to make two panels, each 12" x 18". Insert toothpicks along one long edge of foam. *(Photo 1)*

2. Apply glue to one long edge of second piece of foam. Push edges together tightly, forming one 18" x 24" panel and allow to dry. *(Photo 2)*

3. Center foam panel face down on batting. *(Photo 3)*

4. Clip away corners of batting. Wrap batting around foam *(Photo 4)* and pin in place on the back to hold. *(Photo 5)* The batting should be smooth on the front of the foam. *(Photo 6)*

5. Place the batting-covered panel face down and centered on the wrong side of the fabric piece. Wrap three sides of the fabric around the foam to the back and fold at corners to create neat miters. *(Photo 7)* Fold remaining corners neatly and pin to back of foam. *(Photo 8)* Place the pins at angles to secure them. Be sure they don't protrude through front of panel.

DECORATING THE RIBBONS:

Ribbon 1 - 3/4" gold grosgrain

1. Work the cretan stitch down the center of the ribbon. *(Photo 9)*

2. Single stitch a green bugle bead at each stitch tip. *(Photo 10)*

3. Single stitch a size 11 pale orange seed bead between each stitch. (Photo 10)

Ribbon 2 - 1-1/2" ombre, folded in half lengthwise; use the green/orange side
1. Work maidenhair stitch down the center, using variegated orange/yellow/pink embroidery thread. (Photo 11)

2. Single stitch a pink seed bead at end of each maidenhair stitch. (Photo 12)

Ribbon 3 - 1-1/2" ombre folded in half lengthwise; use pink/orange side
1. Work embroidered split stitch in a wavy line down the center, using green variegated thread. (Photo 13)

2. Add beaded lazy daisy stitches, using pink mix seed beads in each valley. (Photo 14)

3. Lazy stitch orange beads on each side of each lazy daisy. (Photo 14) TIP: When moving to the next bead stitch, slide the needle between the ribbon layers to "bury" the long stitch. (Photo 15) If you work a long stitch on the back of the ribbon, your notes and photos could catch on the thread when you use the memo board.

Ribbon 4 - 1-1/2" sheer green folded in half lengthwise
Alternate single stitched size 8 green seed beads and sequin/size 11 green seed bead stacks along the length of the ribbon. TIP: Use quilting clip to hold the crease in the ribbon while beading. (Photo 16)

Ribbon 5 - 1" gold grosgrain
1. Work herringbone stitch along the length of the ribbon, using variegated orange thread. (Photo 17)

2. Fly stitch gold thread in the valleys, catching the point where the orange thread crosses itself with the tail of the fly stitch. Make a second, smaller fly stitch (creating a double fly stitch) in the valley of each fly stitch. (Photo 18)

3. Single stitch an orange bugle in center of each double fly stitch along one side of the ribbon. (Photo 19)

4. Single stitch a copper-lined seed bead in the center of each fly stitch on the opposite side. (Photo 19)

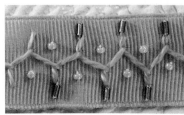

Photo 9 - The cretan stitch embroidered on ribbon 1.

Photo 10 - Beads added to ribbon 1.

Photo 11 - Maidenhair stitch on ribbon 2.

Photo 12 - Single stitched beads at the ends of threads on ribbon 2.

Photo 13 - Split stitch embroidered on ribbon 3.

Photo 14 - Beaded lazy daisies and lazy stitches on ribbon 3.

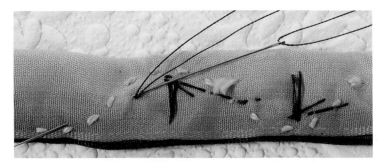

Photo 15 - Back view of ribbon 3: Sliding the needle between the ribbon layers to hide long beading stitches.

Photo 16 - *Alternating single-stitched seed beads and sequin/seed bead stacks. Note the quilting clip that holds the crease in the ribbon.*

Photo 17 - *Herringbone stitches on ribbon 5.*

Photo 18 - *Double fly stitches over the herringbone stitches on ribbon 5.*

Photo 19 - *Single stitch beads along ribbon 5.*

Photo 20 - *Rust cord couched with beads on ribbon 6.*

5. Stitch solid copper seeds on either side of the herringbone stitch intersections. *(Photo 19)*

Ribbon 6 - *1-1/2" sheer copper folded in half*
1. Tack down satin-covered rust cord to make a zig-zag along the length of the ribbon, using gold thread. *(Photo 20)*

2. Couch stitch across the tacks, using three or four small gold seeds. *(Photo 20)*

Ribbon 7 - *1-1/2" ombre, edges folded toward center*
1. Fly stitch, using green variegated thread and catching the edges of the ribbon with the stitching to maintain folds. *(Photo 21)*

2. Single stitch pink bugles at the ends of the stitches along one side. *(Photo 22)*

3. Single stitch green bugle beads at the ends of the stitches along the opposite side. *(Photo 22)*

4. Single stitch copper-lined seed beads down the center between the fly stitches. *(Photo 22)*

Ribbon 8 - *1-1/2" sheer green folded in half lengthwise*
1. Feather stitch down the center, using gold embroidery thread. *(Photo 23)*

2. Single stitch a gold seed bead in each valley. *(Photo 23, Photo 24)*

3. Make a three-bead cluster of green seed beads at end of each stitch. *(Photo 24)*

Ribbon 9 - *1-1/2" sheer copper, edges folded to center*
1. Work a wavy blanket stitch, using variegated orange embroidery thread. *(Photo 25)*

2. Stitch a gold seed at the end of each blanket stitch. *(Photo 25)*

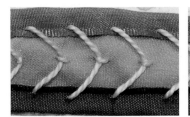

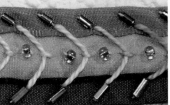

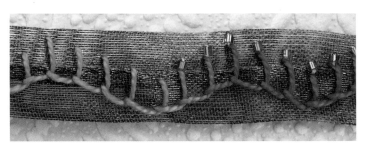

Photo 21 - Fly stitching on ribbon 7.

Photo 22 - Adding single stitched beads to ribbon 7.

Photo 24 - Adding the three-bead clusters to ribbon 8.

Photo 23 - Feather stitching and gold seed beads on ribbon 8.

Photo 25 - A wavy blanket stitch with beads added on ribbon 9.

ASSEMBLY:

1. Following diagram in Fig. A, lay the ribbons at an angle across the fabric-covered board and weave them over and under each other. Use large-head pins to temporarily hold them in place. *(Photo 26)*

2. At each ribbon intersection, push a floral pin through the layers of ribbon and fabric to the back of the board. To make this easier, use a needle tool to make a pilot hole for one leg of the pin. *(Photo 27)* Start the first pin leg in the pilot hole; then use the needle tool to make a pilot hole for the second leg. *(Photo 28)* Carefully push the pin into the board through the pilot holes *(Photo 29)* and press to push the pin all the way through the board. *(Photo 30)*

Photo 26 - Arranged ribbons are pinned to the board.

Photo 27 - Using a needle tool to make a pilot hole for the first leg of a floral pin.

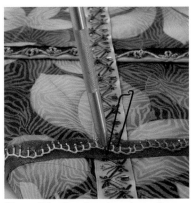

Photo 28 - Starting the pin in first hole and using the needle tool to make a second pilot hole.

Photo 29 - Pushing the pin into the board.

Photo 30 - Pushing the pin all the way into the board.

Photo 31 - At the back of the board, grab the end of the floral pin with pliers and pull.

Photo 32 - Bend the end of the pin against the back of the board.

3. At the back of the board, grasp one leg of the floral pin with needlenose pliers and pull it tightly. (Photo 31) Bend leg of pin toward back of board. (Photo 32) Repeat with the second leg of the floral pin.

4. Glue a leaf bead on each ribbon intersections on the front of the board to cover the floral pins.

5. Use small straight pins to secure the ends of the ribbons to the back of the board, pushing the pins in at an angle. Take care that the sharp ends don't poke through the front of the board.

MAKING THE HANGERS:

1. Cut a 12" to 14" length of wire. Fold in half. (Photo 33)

2. Twist the wire to form a loop at the folded end. (Photo 34)

3. Bend the ends of the wire tails to form hooks. (Photo 35)

4. Repeat to make second wire hanger.

5. Insert hangers into back of memo board near top edge, pressing the hook ends into the foam board. (Photo 36) ✿

Photo 33 - Wire folded in half.

Photo 34 - Wire twisted to form a loop.

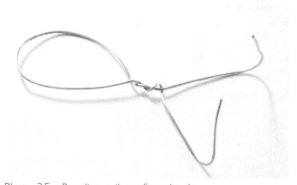

Photo 35 - Bending tails to form hooks.

Photo 36 - Pressing the hooks into the top of the back of the board.

Supplies

PROJECT SURFACE:
• Blue jeans

BEADS:
• 1 tablespoon small pearls - Pale pink
• 2 strands size 2 bugle beads - Mauve
• 1 tablespoon size 11 seed beads - Topaz
• Size 11 seed beads - Pink, bronze, fuchsia
• 2 teaspoons size 15 seed beads - Dark magenta
• Size 15 seed beads - Orange, gold
• Size 6 seed beads - Pink-lined

THREAD & RIBBON:
• 4 mm silk embroidery ribbon - 9 yds. yellow-orange,
  6 yds. salmon, 3 yds. gold
• Size 8 pearl cotton embroidery - Gold
• Size 5 pearl cotton embroidery - Red-violet,
  variegated yellow/orange/magenta
• Beading thread - Dark

TOOLS & OTHER SUPPLIES:
• Beading needle
• Embroidery needle
• Scissors

Stitches Used

See the "Stitching Basics" section for
instructions unless otherwise noted.

EMBROIDERY STITCHES:
• Blanket Stitch - *See Fig. A.*
• Running Stitch - *See Fig. B.*
• Fly Stitch - *See Fig. C.*
• Chain Stitch

BEADING STITCHES:
• Single Stitch
• Bugles Bookended with Seed Beads - *See Fig. D.*
• Beaded Backstitch
• Bead Rings
• Couch with Beads - *See Fig. E.*
• Bead Loops

Jazzed Up Jeans

Breathe new life into your favorite jeans! A little embroidery and beading will transform them into wearable art. TIP: concentrate on the easy-to-reach areas such as hems and pockets; it's tricky to get into the narrow areas around the knees.

Jeans should be hand-washed and gently dried to preserve your stitching. Be sure to check the beadwork and make repairs as necessary after wearing and laundering.

Silk Ribbon Embroidery

For Best Results
- Press silk ribbon with iron on low silk setting prior to stitching to remove creases caused by packaging.
- Use 18" to 24" lengths of silk ribbon with embroidery needle. Knot off and reload needle with ribbon as needed.
- Construct stitches in the same way you would using embroidery thread, but don't pull ribbon as snugly as you would thread--allow the silk ribbon to lay on top of the fabric, keeping the ribbon as flat as possible.

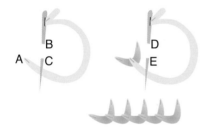

Fig. A - Blanket Stitch
Bring up needle at A, take back down at B, and bring back up at C, keeping ribbon under the point of the needle. Pull up slack to form the stitch.

Start the next stitch by taking the needle down at D, up at E. Repeat for each stitch. End by coming up at D as usual, cross over, and take back down right next to the ribbon at the bend.

Fig. B - Running Stitch
This is as simple as 1-2!
Bring up needle at A, and take it down at B. Keep going up and down, making a straight stitch each time. Keep the lengths of the stitches and the spaces between them consistent or vary the lengths for interest.

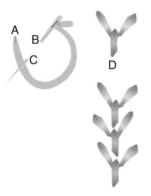

Fig. C - Fly Stitch
Work this stitch just like an embroidered fly stitch.
Bring up the needle at A, take back down at B, and bring back up at C, keeping the ribbon under the point of the needle and as flat as possible. Go back down at D

Instructions

You can do the stitching in any order you like. You may find it easier to use the pattern as a guide and do the stitching freehand rather than transferring the patterns and following them exactly.

RIGHT LEG:

1. Blanket stitch a large spiral, using yellow-orange silk embroidery ribbon. (Fig. A) TIP: When stitching, start at the center of the spiral and work along the pattern line.

2. Single stitch a size 6 pink-lined bead at the end of each blanket stitch.

3. Single stitch a size 15 orange seed bead on top of the silk ribbon connecting each blanket stitch.

4. Stitch a bookended bugle bead border (Fig. D) along the blanket stitching consisting of a size 15 orange seed, a bugle, and another size 15 orange seed bead, leaving 1/8" between the stitches.

Fig. D - Bugles Bookended with Seed Beads - Side view

5. Fly stitch a secondary spiral motif using red-violet pearl cotton.

6. Single stitch a size 11 fuchsia seed bead at the end of each fly stitch.

7. Backstitch branches using bronze size 11 seed beads.

Upper Left Leg Pattern
Enlarge 200% for actual size.

LEFT LEG:

1. Stitch radiating lines from edge of pocket into leg using gold silk ribbon and long running stitches (Fig. B).

2. Stitch small bead rings between each silk ribbon running stitch using 12 size 11 topaz beads.

3. Chain-stitch a wavy, loopy line from the pocket edge down into the leg using size 5 variegated pearl cotton.

4. Blanket stitch around some of the curves using size 8 gold pearl cotton.

5. Single-stitch size 15 gold seed beads at the ends of each blanket stitch.

6. Fly stitch several branches from the lower portion of the leg to the hem using salmon silk embroidery ribbon (Fig. C).

7. Single stitch a small pink pearl at the base of each Y-stem.

8. Single stitch a pink seed bead at the end of each arm.

9. Starting just below the knee, work a fly stitch branch design angled toward the inside seam using variegated pearl cotton.

Lower Left Leg Pattern Enlarge 200% for actual size.

10. Couch (Fig. E) across the end of each Y-stem using four or five size 15 dark magenta seeds.

Fig. E - Couch with Beads - Side view

11. Stitch a tiny bead loop at the end of each Y-arm, using seven dark magenta seeds.

Lower Left Leg Pattern
Enlarge 235% for actual size.

Pint-Size Princess Outfit

A basic outfit becomes something quite special with the addition of embroidery and beads! You'll have as much fun embellishing this top and skirt as the lucky little girl has wearing them. The colors of the shirt made the bead/thread palette choices easy, but don't be afraid to change them to your little princess' favorite colors.

Once you start looking at off-the-rack garments with an eye for embellishment opportunities, you'll see a whole world of wonderful surfaces to which you can add a special accent. The skirt's tiers of ruffles offered several places for adding embroidered borders. This skirt came with a satin extension at the hem, but you could easily add one to a skirt that didn't already have it.

For best results, purchase a top like this one with a V-neck that will slip easily over the child's head without much neckline stretching—the embroidery won't give as much as the t-shirt material.

Size 8 orange beads, size 11 color-lined pink beads.

Pink embroidery thread, beading thread, size 15 orange seed beads.

Size 11 orange and pink beads; orange embroidery thread.

Supplies

PROJECT SURFACE:
- Child's shirt and skirt

BEADS:
- 18 grams *each* size 11 seed beads - Color-lined pink, silver-lined orange, silver-lined pink
- 10 grams size 8 hex-cut seed beads - Silver-lined orange
- 10 grams size 15 seed beads - Silver-lined orange

THREAD:
- Size 8 pearl cotton embroidery thread - Orange
- Size 5 pearl cotton embroidery thread - Pink
- Beading thread - Dark color, pink

TOOLS & OTHER SUPPLIES:
- 3/4" adhesive dots (from office supply store)
- Beading needle
- Embroidery needle

Stitches Used
See the "Stitching Basics" section for instructions.

EMBROIDERY STITCHES:
• Cretan Stitch
• Feather Stitch
• Lazy Daisy Stitch
• Zig-zag Chain Stitch

BEADING STITCH:
• Single Stitch (seed beads)

Skirt Instructions
The borders may be worked in any order you like. Use dark colored beading thread for the beadwork on the skirt.

BEAD SWAGS:
1. Mark two dots at 3 o'clock and 9 o'clock on two stickers. Label the stickers "1" and "2." Locate the center front of the skirt. Place the #1 marked dot at the center front of the skirt hem. Place the #2 dot to the right of the first one, leaving approximately 1/8" between them.
   (Photo 1)

2. Anchor dark thread at the back of the hem and bring to the front next to the left side of the first dot, aligning it with the 9 o'clock mark.

Photo 1 - Sticker dots placed at center front of skirt hem.

Photo 2 - Bead scallop stitched using stickers as guides.

Photo 3 - Second beaded scallop in progress; first dot moved to right.

Photo 4 - Scallops stitched to the right side seam; thread knotted off.

3. Pick up one orange size 8 hex bead and enough color-lined pink beads to reach to the 3 o'clock mark at the right side of the dot, making a beaded swag. Add one more orange hex bead and stitch into the skirt hem between the dots.

4. Make a small stitch at the back of the hem and bring the needle to the front at the top of the last hex bead. Take the needle through the hex bead and two pink beads and emerge between the second and third pink beads. *(Photo 2)*

5. Reposition the first dot to the right of the second dot. Pick up enough beads to go around the dot to the other side, then add a hex bead and stitch into hem. *(Photo 3)*

6. Continue to make beaded swags, moving the stickers as you go, until you reach the side seam of the skirt. Knot off at the back of the hem. *(Photo 4)*

7. Reposition the dots at center front *(Photo 5)* and repeat the process to make bead swags to other side seam.

8. Make bead swags around the back of skirt in the same manner. TIP: If the dots lose their stickiness, mark some new ones to replace them.

CRETAN STITCH BORDER:
1. Work the cretan stitch along the hem of the ruffle, using orange embroidery thread. *(Photo 6)*

2. Single stitch silver-lined pink seeds at the ends of cretan stitches. *(Photo 7)*

3. Single stitch orange size 11 seed beads between each cretan stitch. *(Photo 7)*

Photo 5 - Reposition dots at center front of hem.

Photo 6 - Cretan stitch worked around hem of ruffle.

Photo 7 - Seed beads single stitched onto the cretan-stitched border

Photo 8 - Feather-stitched border just above the bead swags.

FEATHER STITCH BORDER:

1. Feather stitch a border above the bead swags using pink embroidery thread. (Photo 8)

2. Using orange thread, stitch two lazy daisies at the top ends of feather stitches. (Photo 9)

3. Single stitch a silver-lined pink bead at bottom ends of the feather stitches. (Photo 10)

4. Single stitch a color-lined pink bead in each feather stitch cup. (Photo 11)

5. Single stitch a size 11 orange bead at the top of each feather stitch where the lazy daisies join it. (Photo 11)

6. Single stitch size 15 orange beads at the end of each lazy daisy stitch.

CHAIN STITCH BORDER:

1. Using pink embroidery thread, stitch a zig-zag chain around the top of the ruffle. (Photo 12)

2. Single stitch a silver-lined pink bead in the loop of each chain stitch.

3. Single stitch size 15 orange beads in staggered row above the chain-stitched border.

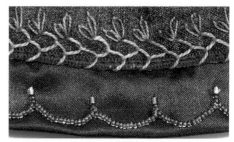

Photo 9 - Lazy daisy stitches added to the feather-stitched border.

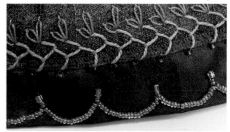

Photo 10 - Pink seed beads added to bottom ends of the feather-stitched border.

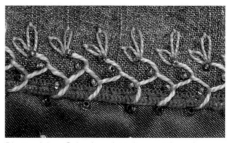

Photo 11 - Color-lined pink seed beads added to the feather-stitched cups; orange size 11 seed beads to the feather-stitched top ends.

Photo 12 - Zig-zag chain stitch added at the top of the ruffle.

Shirt Instructions

Use pink beading thread for the beadwork
on the shirt.

1. Using orange thread, work a row of feather stitching around the neckline. *(Photo 1)*

2. Using pink thread, stitch two lazy daisies at the end of each feather stitch. *(Photo 2)*

3. Single stitch a color-lined pink seed bead at the end of each lazy daisy stitch.

4. Single stitch a silver-lined pink bead at each intersection of the feather and lazy daisy stitches.

5. Single stitch a size 15 orange bead in each feather stitch cup and at the end of each feather stitch that's closer to the neck opening.

6. Use pink thread to make row of cretan stitches around the bottom of each sleeve.

7. Single stitch a silver-lined pink bead between each stitch.

8. Single stitch a size 15 orange bead at the end of each cretan stitch that's closer to the bottom edge of the sleeve.

9. At the opposite side of each cretan stitch, stitch two size 15 orange beads at end of each stitch.

Photo 1 - Feather stitching around the neck of the shirt.

Photo 2 - Lazy daisies stitched at the ends of feather stitches.

The cloth purse as purchased.

Evening Elegance Purse

Bead mixes can supply a variety of coordinated beads for a particular color scheme. You can purchase bead mixes or make your own. Making your own affords the opportunity to combine and use small amounts of beads left over from other projects.

Supplies

PROJECT SURFACE:
• Cloth purse with cord and bead strap

BEADS:
• Glass mini bead mix - Topaz (includes rocailles in assorted sizes and seed beads in light and dark shades)
• Size 5 rocailles - Topaz
• Size 11 seed beads, luster finish - Topaz, dark red
• Size 2 bugle beads - Bright gold
• Assorted decorative glass beads (round, heart, oval)

THREAD:
• Bead-like yarn - Gold
• Sewing thread - Gold metallic
• Beading thread - Rust colored

TOOLS & OTHER SUPPLIES:
• Beading needle
• Tissue paper
• Straight pins
• Small sharp scissors
• Sewing needle

Stitches Used
See the "Stitching Basics" section for instructions.

BEADING STITCHES:
• Backstitch
• Bugles with Seed Beads
• Bead Stack
• Lazy Stitch
• Single Stitch

Photo 1 - Pattern pinned to purse.

Instructions

EMBROIDERING THE OUTLINE:
1. Trace pattern onto tissue paper. Pin the tissue paper tracing to the purse. *(Photo 1)*

2. Drag needle lightly around the central motif to score and/or perforate the tissue paper and again 3/8" away. (The second score gives you a guideline for the size of the loops; both scores make it easier to remove tissue later.)

3. Cut a 24" length of gold bead-like yarn. Tack one end to the pattern line. Make a small loop from the yarn and tack it to the purse on top of the tissue paper pattern. Make another loop the same size right next to the first one and tack in place. Continue making and tacking loops around the motif. *(Photo 2)*

4. Tack the bead-like yarn to the remaining pattern lines, taking extra stitches at ends to secure it tightly. Carefully tear away the tissue paper pattern. *(Photo 3)*

UPPER MOTIF:

1. Backstitch decorative beads in a vertical row down the center of the main motif. *(Photo 4)*

2. Fill in the main motif with lines of gold bugles and pale gold topaz seeds sewn at an angle. *(Photo 4)*

3. Backstitch a row of bead stacks (a rocaille held in place with a seed bead) down the centers of the two leaf-shaped motifs.

4. Fill in around the bead stacks with angled bugles and seeds worked in lazy stitches, backstitches, and single stitches—choose the stitch and beads to fit the size of the space you need to fill. *(See the project photo.)*

5. Where the "leaves" join the "stems," stitch a small round decorative bead with four or more short tassel stems. (The round bead serves as the base for the tassels, which are long bead stacks.) To make the first tassel stem, pick up the round bead and several seeds. Go back through all but the last seed bead and take a stitch into the fabric. Come back up through the round bead and pick up several more seeds. Go back through all but the last seed, go through the round bead, and stitch into the fabric. Come back through round bead each time you start and end a tassel stem.

6. Stitch larger round beads—each held in place with a small seed bead—where the "leaf" joins the "stem."

7. Stitch rocaille-seed bead stacks around the outer edges of the curves.

LOWER MOTIF:

1. Stitch a large oval decorative bead at the center of the lower motif.

2. Embellish with bead stacks--each stack consists of a size 8 seed bead at the base and three size 11 seed beads.

3. At the bottom of the motif, stitch a dangle consisting of a size 8 seed bead, a decorative bead, and four size 11 seed beads.

BOTTOM EDGE:

1. Locate the center of the bottom edge. Stitch a strand of beads to make a 1-3/4" dangle of rocailles, seeds, and decorative beads.

2. Anchor the thread and bring the needle out of the fabric next to the dangle. Work loop-dangle fringe from center to one edge:

For the loop: Pick up ten seed beads, one rocaille, and ten seed beads. Stitch into the fabric 1/2" from the anchor stitch to make the loop.

For the dangle: Pick up a rocaille, a bugle, a seed, a bugle, a seed, a bugle, a seed, a rocaille and a seed. Go back through all but the last seed bead and stitch into fabric. Bring needle back out of purse edge next to last stitch.

Alternate loops and dangles to edge, ending with shorter loop at the corner. Anchor and knot off.

3. Re-anchor thread at the opposite side of the center dangle and work loops and dangles to other corner, ending with a shorter loop. 〰

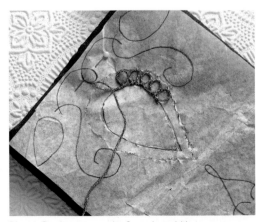

Photo 2 - Loops made from bead-like yarn.

Photo 3 - *The yarn tacked in place, with the tissue paper pattern removed.*

Photo 4 - *The central motif filled in with beadwork.*

Pattern

Bead Crusted Tissue Holder

Imagine carrying around this opulent little accessory in your purse and enjoying it wherever you go.
Encrusting a surface solidly with beadwork makes it feel (and look) like a piece of fine jewelry.

Supplies

PROJECT SURFACE:
• Fabric tissue holder

BEADS:
• Size 11 seed beads - Purple, gray, topaz
• Size 6 rocailles - Burgundy
• Size 15 seed beads - Silver-lined gold
• 3/16" bugle beads - Matte blue
• 1/4" bugle beads - Iris-finish blue/green
• 3/4" twisted bugle beads - Blue
• Accent bead mix (8 mm flower and round beads, 1/2" disc bead)
• 1/4" heart accent bead

THREAD:
• Beading thread - Dark

TOOLS & OTHER SUPPLIES:
• Quilter's transfer pencil
• Beading needle

Tissue holder as purchased.

The beads.

Stitches Used

See the "Stitching Basics" section unless otherwise noted.

BEADING STITCHES:
• Single Stitch (bugle)
• Backstitch (6 beads per stitch)
• Backstitch (alternating bugles and seeds)
• Bead Stack
• Couch around Flower *Bead - See Fig. A.*
• Bugle Rays with Seed Bead Ends - *See Fig. B.*

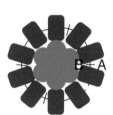

Fig. A - Couch around Flower Bead - Birds eye view
Stitch a flower bead in place. Bring up needle through fabric next to the flower bead and pick up enough seed beads to encircle the flower bead. Take the needle back through the fabric. (**Option:** Go through a few of the first beads on the ring before going into fabric.) Bring up the needle at A just outside the ring of beads. Take the needle across the thread, forming the ring, and down inside the ring at B. Stitch at several points around bead ring.

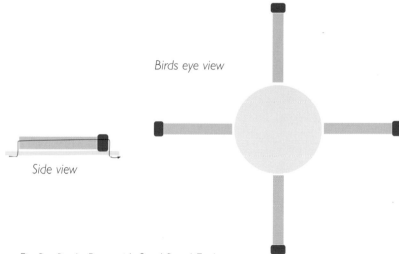

Birds eye view

Side view

Fig. B - Bugle Rays with Seed Bead Ends
Sew a disc bead in place. Bring up thread through the fabric at 12 o'clock position on disc bead and pick up a bugle and a seed. Go back down near the seed bead. Move the needle at the back of the fabric and come up next to disc bead at 3 o'clock. Repeat the bugle/seed bead combination. Work around the disc bead, first stitching the four quadrants. Add three bugle/seed arms in each quadrant. (The seed beads at the ends of the bugles help prevent the thread from rubbing against the bugle's sharp edges.)

Photo 1 - Use a quilter's pencil to draw a guideline for beading.

Photo 2 - First row of bugles completed.

Photo 3 - Seed beads backstitched next to bugle beads.

Instructions

1. Using a quilter's pencil, draw a wavy line across both halves (on either side of opening) of the tissue holder to use as a stitching guide for a row of beads. *(Photo 1)*

2. Single stitch 1/4" bugle beads side by side along the line. *(Photo 2)*

3. Backstitch purple seed beads along both edges of the bugle bead row. *(Photo 3)*

4. Sew short bead stacks–a rocaille plus a purple seed bead–in a few random spots in the lower right corner of the holder and along the left edge of the bead row. *(Photo 4)*

5. Next to the bead stack row, backstitch alternating purple seed beads and matte bugle beads in a row. *(Photo 4)*

6. Stitch a few flower beads and a disc bead in the lower right corner of the holder. *(Photo 4)*

7. Couch a ring of purple seed beads around two flower beads (Fig. A).

8. Backstitch black seeds along right edge of original row. *(Photo 5)*

9. Backstitch additional concentric rings around the flower beads. *(Photo 5)*

10. Stitch twisted bugles plus purple seeds (Fig. B) radiating from the disc bead. Start with rays at 12 o'clock, 3 o'clock, 6 o'clock, and 9 o'clock, then stitch three additional rays in each quadrant. *(Photo 6)*

11. Add an 8 mm round bead and a small heart-shaped bead next to the ringed flower beads. Stitch rings around them as well.

12. Work in a row of matte bugles and add more rings.

13. Fill in between the bugle rays with topaz colored seeds, leaving a little open space so the fabric shows near the right edge of the holder.

14. Extend the bead stacks, matte bugles, and black seeds to the original row of beads on the other half of the holder. *(Photo 7)*

15. Continue stitching "rays" of topaz seeds on the other side of the holder. *(Photo 8)*

16. Backstitch size 15 gold seed beads on the unbeaded area of the holder, following the woven design in the fabric. *(Photo 8)*

17. Stitch a few short rays of black and purple seeds extending from the original row at the lower left of the holder. *(Photo 8)* ✂

Photo 4 - Bead stacks added along the bead row and randomly at lower right; flower beads and disc bead added; bugle row started next to row of bead stacks.

Photo 5 - Black seeds backstitched to right of bugle bead row; couched ring and backstitched rings around flower beads.

Photo 7 - Fill in around bugle rays and flower beads; extend row of stacks and bugles to other half of holder.

Photo 6 - Stitch twisted bugles around the disc bead to make rays.

Photo 8 - Ray extensions on other half of holder; woven pattern outlined with gold seeds; short rays added at left of main row.

Superstar Pouch

A little zippered pouch is handy for holding all sorts of things in a purse, suitcase, or glove box. Purchase an inexpensive one and make it special with bead embroidery—easy and impressive! It makes a great functional gift for any occasion.

The pouch I bought had small foil mirrors on one side. That side became the back; the beaded stars were worked on the other (plain) side. Patterns are provided for the star motifs; you also could use stencils to make the star outlines or draw them freehand.

Supplies

PROJECT SURFACE:
- Purchased zipper pouch with one plain side (Any size will work; mine is 4" x 7".)

BEADS:
- 1 tablespoon size 11 seed beads - Silver-lined gold
- 2 strands size 11 seed beads - Metallic pink

THREAD:
- Beading thread – Dark **or** color to complement your pouch

TOOLS & OTHER SUPPLIES:
- Tracing paper
- Pencil
- White transfer paper
- Stylus
- Beading needle

Stitch Used
See the "Stitching Basics" section for instructions.

BEADING STITCH:
- Beaded Backstitch

The beads.

Photo 1 - Transferred large star motif.

Photo 2 - Knot in center of star motif; shape outlined with rows of pink and gold backstitched beads.

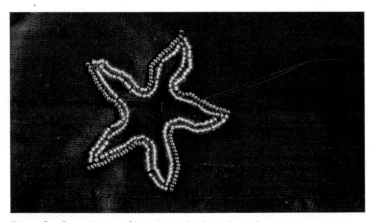

Photo 3 - Second row of beads stitched inside outline.

Instructions

1. Trace the patterns for the stars. Transfer the large star to the pouch. *(Photo 1)*

2. Place the thread knot in the center of the star shape, take needle into pouch, and bring back out at inside corner of star. (The knot will be hidden by the beadwork and will get less wear on the outside of the pouch.) *(Photo 2)*

3. Work the beaded backstitch along the line, alternating lines of pink and gold beads. *(Photo 2)*

   For more control over the shape of the beaded motif: Use shorter beaded backstitches—four or even three beads per stitch. For a four-bead stitch, go back through one or two beads in the second part of the stitch. For three-bead stitches, go back through the last bead in the second part of the stitch.

4. Work a second row of backstitched beads inside the outlined design, using all gold beads. *(Photo 3)* As you work, knot off and start new thread on the outside of the pouch in a spot that will eventually be covered with beads.

5. Continue working concentric rows of beaded backstitches to fill in the star shape. REMINDER: Using fewer than six beads per backstitch (try four or three) will give you more control over the shape of the star.

6. Backstitch rays along the pink parts of the outline, making the rays shorter toward the ends of the pink parts and longer at the center. *(Photo 4)*

7. Transfer a second, smaller star. *(Photo 4)*

8. Outline and fill in the second star with beads, using the same stitching techniques and colors used for the first (large) star. *(Photo 5)*

9. Transfer a third star the same size as the second. Bead the same way.

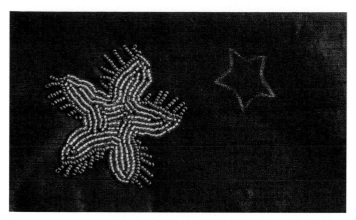

Photo 4 - Large star with rays completed; second star transferred.

Photo 5 - Second star completed.

Patterns

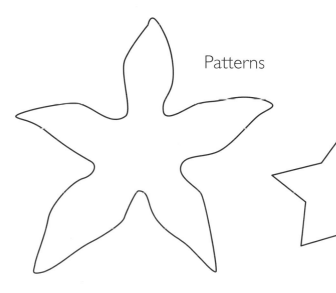

Supplies

PROJECT SURFACE:
• Denim purse with woven flap

BEADS:
The length of a strand of size 11 beads is longer than a size 15 strand.
• 3 strands size 11 opaque seed beads - Purple
• 2 strands size 15 opaque seed beads - Chartreuse
• Size 11 opaque seed beads - Orange
• Size 8 opaque seed beads - Chartreuse, yellow

THREAD:
• Size 5 pearl cotton embroidery - Purple
• Beading thread - Dark

TOOLS & OTHER SUPPLIES:
• Tracing paper
• Pencil
• White transfer paper
• Stylus
• Beading needle

Glitzy Denim Purse

Embellish a simple purse as a gift for your favorite teenager. This one, a denim pouch with a shoulder strap, has a woven fabric flap. Instructions start on page 110.

Stitches Used
See the "Stitching Basics" section for instructions.

EMBROIDERY STITCHES:
• Fly Stitch
• Feather Stitch

BEADING STITCHES:
• Beaded Backstitch
• Bead Stack
• Lazy Stitch
• Single Stitch
• Loops

Purse as purchased.

Beads and thread.

Photo 1 - Star design transferred.

Photo 2 - Using beaded backstitches to outline the design.

Photo 3 - Filling in the star with concentric rows of beads.

Instructions

LARGE STAR:

1. Trace star pattern and transfer to purse, using white transfer paper. *(Photo 1)*

2. Use beaded backstitch to outline the star with purple seed beads. *(Photo 2)*

3. Work concentric rows of backstitched beads to fill in star shape. *(Photo 3)*

4. Backstitch veins of size 15 green beads, placing them on top of the purple beadwork. *(Photo 4)*

5. Stitch bead stacks of size 8 yellow seed beads held in place with size 15 green seed beads around one side of each arm of the star. *(Photo 4)*

SHOOTING STAR SHAPE:

1. Transfer the shooting star motif to the purse. *(Photo 5)*

2. Outline and fill in the shooting star using size 15 green seed beads. *(Photo 6)*

3. Stitch a single purple bead in the center of the shooting star. *(Photo 6)*

4. Backstitch rays with purple seed beads. *(Photo 6)*

5. Extend a curved row of bead stacks from the large star to the edge of the purse. *(Photo 6)*

FLAP EMBROIDERY:

1. Fly stitch a spiral shape with a long tail that crosses the front of the flap, using purple pearl thread. *(Photo 7)*

2. Feather stitch a second line of embroidery on flap, using purple pearl thread. *(Photo 7)*

Photo 4 - Backstitched veins and bead stacks.

Photo 5 - Large star completed; shooting star transferred.

Photo 6 - Shooting star beaded; bead stacks continued.

FLAP BEADING:

1. Lazy stitch orange seed beads at the ends of the fly stitches. *(Photo 8)*

2. Single stitch purple seed beads at the end of each fly stitch. *(Photo 8)*

3. Stitch small bead loops with size 15 green seed beads at the end of each feather stitch. *(Photo 8)*

4. Stitch bead stacks spaced 3/8" apart around the edge of the flap. Alternate stack A and stack B. *(Photo 8)*

   Stack A - Start with one size 8 yellow seed bead, add six orange seeds and one purple seed, go back through the orange and yellow beads, and stitch into flap.

   Stack B - Start with one size 8 green, add six purple seed beads and one orange seed bead, go back through the purple and green beads, and stitch into flap.

BEADING ON EDGE OF PURSE:

Stitch bead stacks of consisting of three beads in alternating color combinations around the body of the purse *(Photo 9)*, spacing the stacks 3/8" apart:

   Stack A - One size 8 green, one size 11 orange, one size 15 green.

   Stack B - One size 8 yellow, one size 11 purple, and one size 15 green.

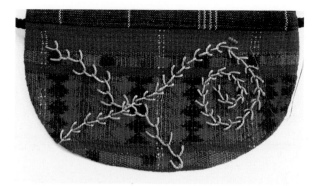

Photo 7 - Embroidery on flap.

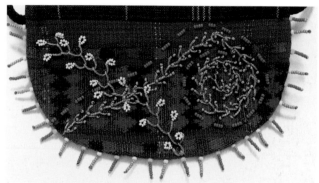

Photo 8 - Beadwork added to flap.

Photo 9 - Adding bead stacks around the edge of the body of the purse.

Patterns

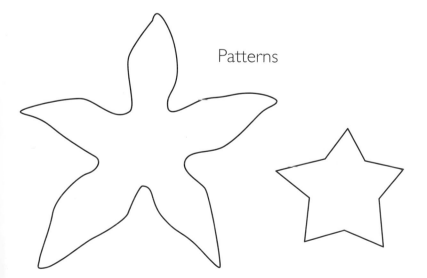

111

Supplies

PROJECT SURFACE:
• Drawstring pouch, approximately 5"

BEADS:
• Size 11 seed beads - Metallic gold, clear cranberry, opaque cranberry
• 8 mm round beads - Metallic gold
• 4 mm hexagonal beads - Metallic gold
• Bugle beads - Metallic gold

THREAD & BRAID:
• Size 8 metallic fine braid - Gold
• Beading thread
• *Optional:* Sewing thread - Metallic gold (This thread is fussier to work with than beading thread.)

TOOLS & OTHER SUPPLIES:
• Beading needle
• Embroidery needle
• Ruler

Precious Possessions Pouch

The woven design of the fabric of this pouch offered lots of options for embellishing, and the deep burgundy stripes and gold metallic threads guided my choices for the embroidery thread and beads.

Stitches Used
See the "Stitching Basics" section for instructions unless otherwise noted.

EMBROIDERY STITCH:
• Fly Stitch

BEADING STITCHES:
• Bugles with Seed Beads
• Lazy Stitch
• Bead Bridge (Dimensional Lazy Stitch) - *See Fig. A.*
• Single Stitch
• Bead Stack - *See Fig. B.*
• Picot Edging - *See Fig. C.*

The pouch as purchased.

Beads and threads.

Instructions

BEADING ON THE POUCH:

Work steps 1, 2, and 3 in the order listed. The rest of the beadwork can be completed in any order.

1. Embroider a row of horizontal side-by-side fly stitches, using gold fine braid and keeping the tail portions of the stitches short. *(Photo 1)*

2. Stitch a bugle bead and a clear cranberry seed bead at the bottom of each fly stitch, using gold metallic sewing thread, if you like. Pick up one bugle bead and one seed bead per stitch. *(Photo 1)* Note: Since the fly stitches at each end of the row were close to the curved bottom of the pouch, a seed bead only—without a bugle bead—was used to begin and end the row.

3. Single stitch a gold seed bead at the top of each fly stitch. *(Photo 1)*

4. Below the row of beaded fly stitching, work a row of five-bead lazy stitches, using opaque cranberry seed beads.

5. Above the row of beaded fly stitching, work a row of vertical bead bridges (Fig. A), using seed beads (four opaque cranberry, one gold, four opaque cranberry for each bridge).

6. Above the bead bridges, stitch 8 mm round gold beads held in place with cranberry seeds. Space them 1/4" apart.

7. Below the drawstring, single stitch gold seed beads. Space them 1/8" apart.

BEADING AT THE BOTTOM & TOP:

1. Around the bottom of the pouch in the seam, stitch 4 mm hexagonal gold beads held in place with cranberry seed beads. Space them 1/4" apart.

2. Around the top edge of the pouch in the seam, stitch bead stacks (Fig. B) using one hexagonal gold bead and four cranberry seed beads. Space them 1/4" apart.

BEADING ON THE DRAWSTRING TABS:

1. At the outer edge of one drawstring tab, stitch a picot edging (Fig. C). Use two cranberry seed beads, then one gold seed, then two cranberry seeds. Take the stitch into the fabric and come back out through the last two cranberry seed beads. Pick up one gold seed and two cranberry seeds. Repeat across edge.

2. Repeat on the remaining drawstring tabs.

Photo 1 - Fly stitching across pouch, with bugle and seed beads added.

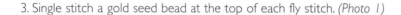

Fig. A - Bead Bridge - Side View

Fig. B - Bead Stack - Side View

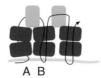

A B
Fig. C - Picot Edging - Side View

Pattern for Night Moves Poncho
Pictured on page 117.
Instructions begin on following page.

Enlarge 200% for actual size.

Back

Front

Shoulder

The poncho as purchased.

Beads, heat-set crystals, and heat-set tool.

Supplies

PROJECT SURFACE:
• Poncho

BEADS & CRYSTALS:
• 80 grams size 10 iris-finish beads - Green
• 50 size 20 ss heat-set silver-backed clear crystals - Aurora borealis finish

THREAD:
• Beading thread - Dark

TOOLS & OTHER SUPPLIES:
• Tissue paper
• Black permanent marker
• Straight pins
• Crystal heat-set tool
• Beading needle
• Needle tool or seam ripper
• Small paintbrush and container of water
• Tracing paper

Stitch Used
See the "Stitching Basics" section for instructions.

BEADING STITCH:
• Backstitch

See page 115 for pattern.

Night Moves Poncho

A plain black poncho can be transformed into an elegant covering that works as well with evening wear as it does with blue jeans!

Instructions

PREPARATION:
1. Trace pattern on tracing paper and enlarge as directed. Trace the part of the pattern for the right side (as you face the poncho) of the front on tissue paper.

2. Determine and mark the center front and center back of the poncho, then mark the shoulders.

3. Pin the tissue pattern to the poncho between the center front and the right shoulder. *(Photo 1)*

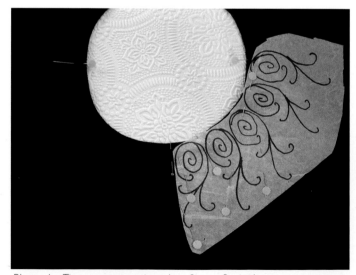

Photo 1 - Tissue pattern pinned to front of poncho.

Photo 2 - Backstitching beads over pattern lines.

Photo 3 - Stitching along the lines of the first motif.

Photo 4 - Continuing to bead the motif.

Photo 5 - Emerging from beads already stitched to connect a new section to an existing one within a motif.

BEADING:

1. Starting on the scroll closest to the center front, work the beaded backstitch with green beads along the pattern lines, stitching through the tissue and poncho fabric. (Photo 2) Continue working sections of the scroll, adding pins as needed to keep the pattern from shifting out of place as you work. As beads are stitched and hold the tissue in place, pins can be removed. (Photo 3) Where one section of the scroll meets another, pass the needle through some of the existing beads for a smooth connection. Work the sections of the scroll in any order you like. (Photo 4) Start the last section of the scroll by running the needle through beads already stitched and emerging from a bead near an intersection on the pattern. (Photo 5)

2. Move to the scroll motif nearest the shoulder and stitch beads over it, following the tissue paper pattern. (Photo 6) Work the sections of the scroll in the order that feels most comfortable. (Photo 7) TIP: When that scroll is completed, many of the pins can be removed and the pattern will stay in place. You can spot pin near the scroll you are working without having extra pins all over the place.

3. Bead the rest of the scrolls, working from the ends toward the center. (Photo 8)

4. When this section of the poncho is completely beaded, carefully tear away the tissue pattern. Because the beading needle will have perforated it, it should tear easily. (Photo 9) TIP: IF you have trouble removing the tissue, soften

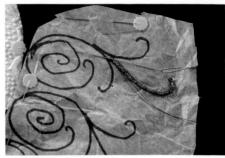

Photo 6 - Moving to the motif closest to the shoulder.

Photo 7 - Working sections of the second motif.

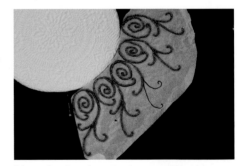

Photo 8 - Beading the last motif in this quadrant.

Photo 9 - Tearing away the tissue when beading is complete.

Photo 10 - The tissue removed.

Photo 11 - Beading the other side of the front of the poncho.

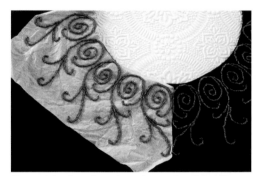

Photo 12 - Beading the back of the poncho in two sections.

it by brushing on a little plain water, using a small paint brush. (Very little moisture is needed.) Wait a few seconds, then pull away the tissue paper. Use a needle tool or the pointy end of a seam ripper to coax little bits of tissue out of the beading thread. Be patient and meticulous and remove all the tissue. *(Photo 10)*

5. Repeat the beading process on the left front side of the poncho. *(Photo 11)*

6. Bead the design on the back of the poncho, working in two sections. *(Photo 12)* When two scrolls are completed on the second half of the back, remove the tissue from the first half. *(Photo 13)* If you wish, remove the tissue around the scrolls as you complete each one. *(Photo 14)*

ADDING THE CRYSTALS:

1. Practice using the heat-setting tool and crystals on a scrap of fabric similar to that of your poncho, following the manufacturer's instructions. Get comfortable using the tool.

2. Attach the crystals to the back of the poncho, using the dots on the pattern as a guide for placement. *(Photo 15)* TIP: Keep a needle tool handy to help push crystals out of the tool if they don't release easily.

3. Affix crystals to the front of the poncho. ❧

Photo 13 - The front and one half of the back is beaded; the tissue paper pattern remains in place on the remaining back half.

Photo 14 - Tissue is removed as beading is completed.

Photo 15 - Crystals affixed to the back of the poncho.

The sandals as purchased.

Seed beads and faceted beads.

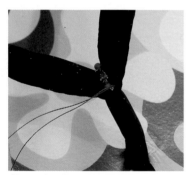

Photo 1 - Start the beading at the center.

Photo 2 - Several rows are beaded; faceted beads are added at the center of every fifth or sixth row.

Supplies

PROJECT SURFACE:
• Sandals or flip flops with fabric straps

BEADS:
• 5 strands size 11 seed beads - Iris-finish blue
• 4 mm faceted blue/black beads

THREAD:
• Beading thread - Dark

TOOLS & OTHER SUPPLIES:
• Sturdy beading needle

Stitch Used

See the "Stitching Basics" section for instructions.

BEADING STITCH:
• Lazy Stitch

Instructions

Follow these instructions to bead each sandal.

1. Anchor the beading thread near the center of the strap. Bring the needle out at one edge. Pick up enough size 11 beads to span the top surface of the strap and take the needle through the opposite side of the strap (the lazy stitch). Slide the needle through the strap and out at the starting position for next bead row. *(Photo 1)*

2. Continue stitching beads across the top of the strap, working toward one side and keeping the rows close together so the strap is completely covered. Every fifth row or so, pick up a 4 mm faceted bead in the middle of the lazy stitch. *(Photo 2)* When you reach the end of the strap, knot off the thread.

3. Go back to center and start a new thread. Work beading on second side of strap. *(Photo 3)*

Bling *on* the Beach Shoes

Next time you're shopping for sandals, pay attention to their construction. Do they have fabric surfaces that will allow beading? This pair had a velvety strap that was easy to stitch into. Keep the beads on top of the strap, though—they wouldn't feel comfortable against your foot!

Photo 3 - One sandal is finished.

Supplies

PROJECT SURFACE:
- Flip flops with wide cloth straps

BEADS:
- 2 strands size 11 seed beads - Pink
- Size 11 seed beads - Orange
- Size 6 rocailles - Pink

THREAD:
- Size 8 pearl cotton - Pink, orange
- Beading thread - Dark

TOOLS & OTHER SUPPLIES:
- Rubber stamp - 1-1/2" triangle spiral
- Fabric paints - Peach, pink
- Paper towel, plastic lid, or disposable plate (for paint palette)
- Non-fusible interfacing, 2" × 8"
- Fusible web, 2" × 4"
- Iron and ironing board
- Parchment paper
- Credit card **or** plastic paint spreader
- Cosmetic sponge (for loading paint on stamp)
- Scissors
- Air-erase fabric marker
- Embroidery needle
- Beading needle
- Sturdy sewing needle

So Sparkly Sandals

Use this idea to transform everyday flip flops into designer footwear. The wide cloth straps on these flip flops offered plenty of room for embroidery and beadwork. I wanted to cover the brown leather-look center sections—beaded medallions do that nicely!

Stitches Used
See the "Stitching Basics" section for instructions unless otherwise noted.

EMBROIDERY STITCH:
- Blanket Stitch

BEADING STITCHES:
- Backstitch (3 beads per stitch) - *See Fig. A.*
- Chain Stitch
- Single Stitch

Instructions

MAKING THE MEDALLIONS:
1. Fold interfacing in half and crease. Apply peach paint to one half, using a credit card or similar device to spread an even coat. Let dry. *(Photo 1)*

The flip flops as purchased.

Spools of pearl cotton thread, beads, stamp, fabric paint.

Photo 1 - Interfacing painted with peach paint.

Photo 2 - The stamp loaded with paint.

Photo 3 - Image stamped on painted interfacing.

Photo 4- Fusing the interfacing layers together.

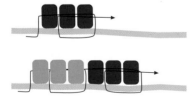

Fig. A - Backstitch with three beads - Side View

2. Squeeze a small amount of pink paint on a palette. Dab the wide end of the cosmetic sponge in the paint. Apply an even coat of the paint to the stamp. *(Photo 2)*

3. Stamp the spiral design on the painted interfacing. Reload the stamp and stamp to make a second image. Let dry. *(Photo 3)*

4. Fold painted interfacing in half at the crease. Place fusible webbing between the interfacing layers. Place the folded interfacing with the webbing between two pieces of parchment paper. Iron to fuse interfacing layers together. *(Photo 4)* Let cool.

5. Anchor beading thread at the back of interfacing. Starting at the outside end of the motif, backstitch pink rocailles, using three beads per stitch (Fig. A) along the lines of the image to start a beaded medallion. *(Photo 5, Photo 6)*

6. Chain stitch size 11 orange beads to fill the space inside the spiral. *(Photo 7)*

7. Chain and single stitch orange seed beads around the outside of the spiral. Note: The decrease from chain to single stitch on the outer edge streamlines the medallion. *(Photo 8)*

8. Carefully trim the interfacing around the beaded medallion near edges of beads, making sure not to clip any of the threads. *(Photo 9. Photo 10)*

9. Stitch a second medallion and trim. Set aside.

Photo 5 - Backstitching the spiral motif with size 6 pink beads.

Photo 6 - The finished spiral.

Photo 7 - Filling in with chain-stitched orange beads.

Photo 8 - The finished medallion.

Photo 9 - The back of the trimmed medallion.

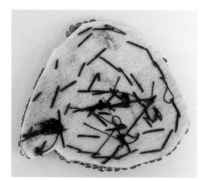

Photo 10 - The front of the trimmed medallion.

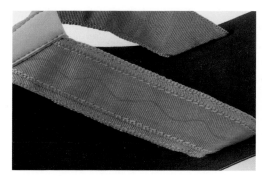

Photo 11 - A wavy line drawn on a strap.

Photo 13 - Blanket stitching a second row with orange thread.

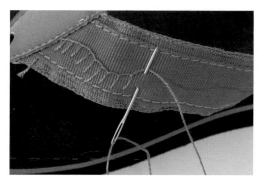

Photo 12 - Blanket stitching along the wavy line.

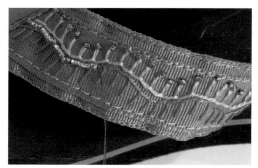

Photo 14 - Single stitched orange beads at ends of blanket stitches; backstitched seed beads between the rows.

EMBROIDERING & BEADING THE STRAPS:

1. Use an air-erase marker to draw a wavy line at the center of one fabric strap. *(Photo 11)*

2. Blanket stitch with pink pearl cotton along the wavy line. *(Photo 12)*

3. Embroider another row of blanket stitching along the wavy line with orange pearl cotton, leaving a small gap between the rows. *(Photo 13)*

4. Single stitch a size 11 orange bead at the end of each orange blanket stitch. *(Photo 14)*

5. Backstitch size 11 pink beads between the blanket stitched rows. *(Photo 14)*

6. Single stitch a size 11 pink bead at the end of each pink blanket stitch.

7. Repeat the steps in this section to embroider and bead the remaining straps of both sandals.

ATTACH THE MEDALLIONS:

1. Using a sturdy sewing needle, anchor the thread at the back of one of the leather-like center sections. Bring the needle to the front. Position and align one beaded medallion over the section and bring needle through from back to front of medallion between the rows of beading. Stitch through all layers to secure the medallion to the sandal. Bring the needle back out and make additional large stitches as needed to hold the medallion securely, hiding the stitches between the rows of beading. Knot off at back of medallion, on the front.

2. Repeat step 1 to attach the other medallion to the other sandal. NOTE: To differentiate the two sandals (since the medallions are identical), turn the second medallion 180 degrees.

Metric Conversions

Inches to Millimeters and Centimeters

Inches	MM	CM
1/8	3	.3
1/4	6	.6
3/8	10	1.0
1/2	13	1.3
5/8	16	1.6
3/4	19	1.9
7/8	22	2.2
1	25	2.5
1-1/4	32	3.2
1-1/2	38	3.8
1-3/4	44	4.4
2	51	5.1
3	76	7.6
4	102	10.2
5	127	12.7
6	152	15.2
7	178	17.8
8	203	20.3
9	229	22.9
10	254	25.4
11	279	27.9
12	305	30.5

Yards to Meters

Yards	Meters
1/8	.11
1/4	.23
3/8	.34
1/2	.46
5/8	.57
3/4	.69
7/8	.80
1	.91
2	1.83
3	2.74
4	3.66
5	4.57
6	5.49
7	6.40
8	7.32
9	8.23
10	9.14

Index